# The Rule of Law
# in South Korea

# The Rule of Law in South Korea

Jongryn Mo

*and*

David W. Brady

*EDITORS*

HOOVER INSTITUTION PRESS
Stanford University   Stanford, California

www.hoover.org

Hoover Institution Press Publication No. 562

First printing, 2010
18　17　16　15　14　13　12　　8　7　6　5　4　3　2

Manufactured in the United States of America

The paper used in this publication meets the minimum requirements of the American National Standard for Information Sciences—Permanence of Paper for Printed Library Materials, ANSI Z39.48-1992.♾

Library of Congress Cataloging-in-Publication Data
Jongryn Mo and David W. Brady, editors
The rule of law in South Korea /
edited by Jongryn R. Mo and David W. Brady
　　　p.　cm. — (Hoover Institution Press publication ; no. 562)
Includes bibliographical references and index.
ISBN-13: 978-0-8179-4892-4 (pbk. : alk. paper)
ISBN-13: 978-0-8179-4896-2 (e-book)
　　1. Rule of law—Korea (South)　2. Law reform—Korea (South).
　　I. Mo, Jongryn, 1961–　　II. Brady, David W.
KPA2020.R85　2010
340'.3095195—dc22　　　　　　　　　　　2009046360

# CONTENTS

# PREFACE

# Jongryn Mo and Chaihark Hahm

The papers contained in this volume were originally presented at the Conference on Democracy, Market Economy, and the Rule of Law in Korea, held in November 2004 at the Hoover Institution on the Stanford University campus. The conference was convened under the joint auspices of the Hoover Institution and Yonsei University. The papers have been revised to cover developments through the end of the Roh Moo Hyun administration (2003–2008).

Scholarly interest in the concept of the rule of law as an ideal for Korean society is not new. It can be traced at least as far back as the 1960s when Korea was one of the poorest countries in the world. Most people then seem to have all but despaired at the enormity of the gap between the ideal of rule of law and the reality of the Korean social and political situation. Today, Korea is a member state of the Organisation for Economic Co-operation and Development (OECD), and is commonly counted as one of the handful of countries that have achieved the dual goal of economic prosperity and political liberalization. Yet many observers still point to the persistent gap between the rule of law and the prevalent practices of Koreans. Unlike economic development or political democratization, the rule of law apparently continues to elude the Korean people. Hence, studies on the rule of law in the Korean context continue to be produced.

Nevertheless, as compared to the previous generations of analysts of Korea, today's scholars are in a better position to assess the status and prospects of the rule of law. This is due in part to better theoretical tools made available through advances in different fields of inquiry, such as law, political science, and developmental studies. In addition, the Korean legal system itself, along with its economy and political structure, has become much more complex, with myriad rules and regulations that simply did not exist half a century ago. In other words, scholars in various disciplines now are able to engage in much more focused, substantive, and empirically-informed studies of the various segments of the Korean society from the perspective of rule of law, rather than engage in general normative discussions about the need to transform the entire Korean society to match some vaguely articulated conception of the rule of law. This partly explains the continuing scholarly attention on the rule of law in Korea. This also means that as Korean law becomes more sophisticated in the future, more studies and analyses of the Korean version of the rule of law will become necessary.

Moreover, this may also mean that the scholarly discourse is now able to move away from the broad appeals for closing the supposed gap between ideal and reality toward more concrete and fruitful investigations of the various parts of the current legal system. It is hoped that the current volume represents such a new development in the discourse on the rule of law in Korea. At the least, it represents a significant departure from the conventional studies on the topic just by virtue of taking an interdisciplinary approach. The chapters are authored not only by lawyers and legal scholars, but also by political scientists and economists, with different outlooks and approaches. Present also at the conference at which the chapters herein were presented were sociologists, practicing attorneys, and specialists from Japan and China. The editors wish to thank all the participants of the conference whose insights and criticism helped to make the event that much more stimulating and meaningful. We particularly wish to thank the presenters and discussants who are not represented in the chapters of this volume: Jennifer Amyx, Jong-Goo Yi, Randall Peerenboom, William Ratliff, Gi-Wook Shin, and Scott Snyder. A special thanks is due the Hon. Lee Hoi-Chang, former prime minister of South Korea and justice of the Supreme Court who, though not present at the conference, graciously agreed to have his paper included in this volume as the lead chapter. We believe that his chapter, significantly enriches the volume by presenting a clear and succinct overview of the debates on the rule of law in relation to the Korean constitution.

We would like to express our appreciation for the Korea Foundation whose grant to the Hoover Institution provided the basis for the project that sponsored the conference. Stephen and Maria Kahng also provided significant support, for which we are most grateful. We also want to thank John Raisian, the Tad and Dianne Taube Director of the Hoover Institution, and Larry Diamond, Charles Wolf Jr., and other members of the Hoover community for their continuing interest and support of this project. The encouragement of Thomas Heller and Gerhard Casper of Stanford Law School was most welcome. We are grateful to the Yonsei Globalization Research Initiative, the Graduate School of International Studies, and its director, Sung-Shin Han, for financially supporting the Yonsei participants. Teresa Judd and Christie Harlick provided much-needed logistical support during the conference. The assistance of Joan D. Saunders during the final stages of editing was invaluable.

INTRODUCTION

# The Elusive Goal of the
# Rule of Law in South Korea

## Jongryn Mo

EAST ASIA has come a long way in the development of democracy and a market economy. As late as 1987, Japan was the only free country in East Asia. By the late 1990s, South Korea and Taiwan had joined the exclusive group of free countries. The story is similar on the economic front. South Korean and Taiwanese market economies have shed their developmental past to such an extent that they have become primarily open economies, both in trade and in finance.

But weak legal systems are clouding East Asia's economic and political future. For evidence, all one has to do is point to the pervasiveness of corruption in all East Asian countries. Corruption seems to be part of every East Asian's daily life, regardless of whether she lives in a mature democracy, a new democracy, or a communist regime. Neither does law seem to restrain executive power. East Asian political leaders and bureaucrats have often been accused of arbitrary exercises of power.

The weak rule of law is also slowing progress toward a market-based economic system.[1] Corporate governance throughout East Asia is opaque and unaccountable. Family control of large enterprises is almost always the norm. Where family control is weak, there is control by informal networks of people or companies instead, not by legal

---

1. "In Praise of Rules," *Economist*, April 5, 2001

representatives of shareholders. Financial markets are also underdeveloped and nontransparent. East Asian regulators still struggle with prudential regulations and insider trading. Accounting transparency is also suspect.

In many parts of East Asia, the rule of law is deteriorating even in the area of law and order. South Korea has had difficulty controlling illegal strikes and demonstrations. Taiwan's biggest problem is organized crime. China suffers from the loss of public control at local government levels (Pei 2002).

## What Is Wrong?

It is a common practice to blame history for the weak rule of law in East Asia. First, traditional paternalistic views of authority emphasize obedience and loyalty to group interests, not advocacy of individual rights. Second, both East Asian leaders and Western colonial rulers in East Asia used the law as an instrument of power, not as a restraint on their own power. The term, the rule of law, is thus associated with coercion, social control, unilateral compliance, and formal legalism. Because of this historical abuse of the law, East Asians are said to believe that the law is for the benefit of the ruler, not the individual.

Although it is important to recognize historical constraints, it is equally important to know where history matters and where it may not. For example, one has to be careful to argue that the weak rule of law has been driven by the belief in the rule of man because there have been strands of East Asian thought emphasizing various elements of the rule of law (Kang 2003).[2] Throughout authoritarian and colonial rules, East Asians also rebelled against arbitrary exercise of

2. Kang points out that the Chinese philosophy of Legalism stresses the first two elements of the modern rule of law, the supremacy of laws and equality before the law. Confucianism, on the other hand, is mainly concerned with the third element of the rule of law, the constitutional problem of how to control rulers. Therefore, one cannot say that the rule of law is alien to East Asian tradition.

power by their rulers, suggesting that they did not share the rulers' view of the rule of law.

One area, however, in which history is very much relevant is the weakness of the belief in the sanctity of the individual person. Although one can find many Confucian teachings consistent with the rule of law, one would be hard-pressed to find support for the primacy of the individual or individual rights in traditional East Asian philosophy.[3] Hahm (1986, 286) elaborates on this point as follows:

> It is difficult to explain the role of an individual in old Korea. The concept of an individual was a very amorphous one. It was not a totalitarian collectivist view of an individual. Nor was it anything analogous to modern individualism of America. In old Korea an individual was always conceptualized as a part of the universe and a part of the universe was represented in the individual. It was not that the individual was never conceptualized as an independent category, but the individual was always considered to be in a partially interlocking or mutually interpenetrating position with other human beings as well as with the Modern World. The individual was always viewed in the context of his affection network. The individual was never viewed as separate and entirely distinct from his blood relations. This is a difficult concept to be grasped by a person with the Western individualist cultural perspectives.

Even now, when public support for the rule of law in East Asia is high, it is questionable whether East Asians truly understand that the rule of law requires a strong commitment to the individual relative to the collective and the primary role of law is to protect individual rights. Park and Kim (1987), for example, find that among democratic principles (human dignity, individualism, liberty, equality, and popular sovereignty), the support for individualism is weakest among Korean elites. Therefore, if an East Asian society wants to achieve the rule of law, it must first respect and protect the individual person (i.e., her dignity, worth, and ability).

---

3. A possible exception may be non-mainstream Taoism.

In a review of basic components of the rule of law, it is easy to see why the sanctity of the individual person is so important to the rule of law. Hager (1999), for example, offers nine conditions for a strong legal system: (1) constitutionalism, (2) law governs the governments, (3) an independent judiciary, (4) law must be fairly and consistently applied, (5) law is transparent and accessible to all, (6) application of the law is efficient and timely, (7) property and economic rights are protected, including contracts, (8) human and intellectual rights are protected, and (9) law can be changed by an established process that itself is transparent and accessible to all. This list is a mixture of principles and institutions designed to realize them. According to Hager, required institutions are a constitution, a limited government, and an independent judiciary. Among the three principles underlying Hager's framework—individual rights (7, 8, 9), equality before the law (4, 5, 9), and efficiency (6)—we can see that the first two are based on respect for the individual rather than for the collective.[4]

To summarize, I argue in this essay that the problem with the rule of law in East Asia is not a lack of public support for it. Neither is it right to say that East Asian tradition is wholly incompatible with the rule of law. The real problem lies in the misunderstanding of what constitutes the rule of law and what its primary goal is. The goal of the rule of law is, first and foremost, to uphold human dignity and worth and protect individual liberty and rights.

Let me now turn to explaining in more detail the three-way relationship between individual rights, the rule of law, and development in an East Asian country at the forefront of institutional change, South Korea.

4. My notion of the sanctity of the individual person in this essay is different from a common definition of individualism, the belief that individual interests prevail over group interests (Hofstede, 1991). It is not right to think of individual rights and group rights as always conflictual. At the level of basic human rights, individual and group interests coincide. It should also be noted that both freedom and equality are concepts based on the respect for the individual person.

## Individual Rights, the Rule of Law, and Democracy

Liberal democracy is a political system that respects the dignity and worth of the individual person and guarantees individual liberty and rights. After observing the demise of totalitarian regimes in imperial Japan and Nazi Germany, the disintegration of the communist system in the Soviet Union and Eastern Europe, and the transformations of European socialist states and parties, one cannot deny that liberal democracy or the choice of liberal democratic values is one of the forces shaping human history.

The history of democratization generally shows that a transition to democracy follows a successful escape from poverty—economic advancement through industrialization. Although some people dismiss as authoritarian the Park Chung Hee regime that achieved remarkable economic growth through industrialization for 20 years, from the early 1960s to the late 1970s, it is an undeniable fact that it laid the foundation for subsequent democratic development by relieving its people of hunger and poverty. Only after people solve their subsistence problem do they start demanding rights to elect their political leaders. These demands, in turn, lead to free election of political leaders as representatives of their people and a legitimate government.

However, holding elections and changing governments through elections do not mean the arrival of a mature democracy. Elections, that is, people's collective decisions, aggregate the decisions of each and every individual. The choice of the individual can be genuinely made only if the individual's dignity and worth are respected and liberty and rights are protected, that is, if basic individual rights such as freedom of expression and right to vote are fully guaranteed. Therefore, where this premise is not satisfied, a mature democracy cannot exist, and worse, an immature democracy could arise, one in which elections are abused as means of populism and demagogy.

What is the condition that leads to the respect for individual dignity and worth and the protection of individual liberty and rights?

It is none other than the rule of law. Law acts as the minimal rule that can protect individual liberty and rights and enable the coordination and harmony of interests between individuals and between the community and the individual. Law will protect individual liberty and rights from illegitimate exercise of state power and the tyranny of individuals and groups. Especially important is the role of law in deterring individuals and groups who interfere with the rightful exercise of state power in promoting individual liberty and rights. Although the primary goal of the rule of law is to protect individual liberty and rights, it is also designed to ensure the rightful exercise of state authority. The basic value of the law with such normative functions is justice. This notion of justice is not different from that of fairness. Therefore, a society in which the rule of law prevails can be called a just and fair society.

## Korean Democracy and the Rule of Law

Korea experienced the rules by two nonelected presidents, Choi Kyu Ha and Chun Doo Hwan, after the collapse of President Park Chung Hee. A constitutional revision paved the way for the direct election of President Roh Tae Woo in 1987, and President Lee Myong Bak is now the fifth president elected under the new constitution after Kim Young Sam, Kim Dae Jung, and Roh Moo Hyun.

Although the period from Park Chung Hee through Roh Tae Woo (except for the brief period under Choi Kyu Ha) is often referred to as the period of military regimes, and the reigns of Kim Young Sam and Kim Dae Jung are called the period of democratizing regimes because of their prodemocracy activities, we can safely say that Korean democracy took its first step during the military regime period because President Chun Doo Hwan kept his promise of a one-term presidency and agreed to the direct election of the president, and Roh Tae Woo was the first directly elected president.

The victory of Kim Dae Jung in the 1997 election as an opposition candidate marked the first time that the ruling party lost and thus was touted as a significant step in democratic consolidation. Some foreign scholars and observers even argued that the election of Kim Dae Jung, who fought for democracy under the threat of assassination under the Park Chung Hee regime, was the evidence for the success of Korean democracy.

In reality, the Kim Dae Jung government bullied opposition parties and other critics, using security and law enforcement agencies such as the National Intelligence Service (NIS) and the Office of Public Prosecutors. Especially noteworthy in this regard is his attempt to suppress the freedom of press by ordering tax investigations of newspapers critical of his government. Security agencies such as the NIS were also implicated in illegal wiretappings and investigations of financial transactions. As a result, it was not unusual to see people using hard-to-tap cellular phones and changing their numbers regularly or preferring to talk in person to discuss sensitive matters.

Moreover, the government at that time did not hesitate to encourage and support actions inconsistent with law and order when they suited their political interests. During the 2000 general elections, the Kim Dae Jung government defended nongovernmental organizations (NGOs) that organized illegal campaigns against opposition candidates and even hinted that the law could be broken if it served a legitimate purpose and cited the student democracy uprising of 1960 as a good example.

Can we say that we live in a period of consolidated democracy when our government violates individual liberty and rights by ignoring laws or manipulating them against the spirit of legal justice? There is no need to say how much one would be ignoring the essence of democracy by calling our time a period of successful democracy simply because the president has a prodemocracy activist background or an opposition party's electoral victory leads to change of government.

One of the salient trends that emerged under the Roh Moo Hyun government is that laws were not enforced according to original intent, and the confusion in law and order aggravated the government's ideologically one-sided and self-serving positions on labor, North Korea, U.S.-Korean relations, and some NGOs and interest groups' defiant behavior in demonstrations and protests. These phenomena, which undermined the realization of justice, one of the values of law, force us to seriously fear the loss of the rule of law.

## Individual Rights, the Rule of Law, and Market Economy

The logic of individual rights that we see in the realization of democracy can be easily transferred to the realm of a market economy. As is true with democracy, the building of a market economy requires the rule of law, which in turn cannot take root without the shared understanding of the need to protect individual rights. Let me first explore the relationship between individual rights and a market economy.

A common definition of a market economy is that it relies on market prices to allocate resources. Defined this way, a market economy is a concept opposite to that of a planned economy in which resources are allocated according to government plans. The difference between a market economy and a planned economy comes down to the number of people making autonomous decisions. In a market economy, every economic agent, whether buyer or seller, makes autonomous decisions, whereas in a planned economy, economic decisions are centralized and concentrated in the hands of a few people.

Why should individuals be allowed to make decisions according to their interests? To the extent market transactions are based on self-interest and information, there is no question that individuals who are parties to market transactions are in the best position to take advantage of them. What is interesting about relying on individual decisions is not that individuals know what is best for them, which is rather obvious. Since Adam Smith, economists' faith in individual choice has come from the claim that economic self-interest ultimately serves the public good through the workings of an invisible hand. In a market economy, private interest thus becomes a public virtue. The only condition necessary for the unleashing of such market forces is the security of property rights that allows individuals to keep the private benefits of their economic activities.

It is fair to say that individual economic freedom is to a market economy what individual liberty and rights are to democracy. The key ingredients of economic freedom are personal choice, voluntary exchange, freedom to compete, and protection of person and property. On the one hand, "governments [in a modern market economy] promote economic freedom when they provide a legal structure and law enforcement system that protects the property rights of owners and enforces contracts in an even-handed manner and facilitate access to sound money." On the other hand, governments "must refrain from actions that interfere with personal choice, voluntary exchange, and the freedom to enter and compete in labor and product markets. Economic freedom is reduced when taxes, government expenditures, and regulations are substituted for personal choice, voluntary exchange, and market coordination. Restrictions that limit entry into occupations and business activities also retard economic freedom" (Fraser Institute 2002).

Before addressing the question of how the protection of individual rights is institutionalized in a modern market economy, let me examine the moral foundation of individual freedom. Free market theorists since Adam Smith have tried to justify economic freedom in terms of economic efficiency. For most of us, however, the morality of economic efficiency is not sufficiently appealing. One reason is that the criterion of economic efficiency that the economists use, Pareto efficiency, does not address the problem of fairness of resource allocations. According to Pareto efficiency, a given distribution of resources is efficient if there is no other allocation that makes everyone better off. Whether or not the original distribution gives everything, or a disproportionably large amount, to one rich person does not affect its efficiency if any alternative distribution involves the reduction of the rich person's holdings, no matter how small that may be.

Because of the limited appeal of the efficiency argument, there have been attempts to defend economic freedom on other philosophic grounds. Two of them deserve attention. The first example is what Weber calls the Protestant ethic. According to Weber, the religious beliefs held by the Protestants about their economic activity explain their superior economic performance over the Catholic societies in the two and a half centuries since the Reformation. The Protestants, especially the Calvinists, believed in the ideal of the calling: God had ordained for each individual a place in the world so that His plan could be carried out. A godly man, therefore, would carry out his role in God's plan diligently and enthusiastically, whatever that role may be. If your role happened to be largely economic, it would be your duty to work diligently and to abstain from excessive consumption. Since people with the Protestant ethic saved more, the Protestant societies with large entrepreneur classes experienced higher rates of accumulation and thus economic growth.

Another attempt to justify economic freedom in moral terms was social Darwinism. Borrowed from the evolutionary theory of Charles Darwin, social Darwinists such as Herbert Spencer and William Sumner viewed market competition as the survival of the fittest and market outcomes as products of a natural selection. Thus, the pursuit of self-interest and fierce competition represent the state of nature, so there is no reason for interfering with such natural process. Implicit in social Darwinism is the assumption that individuals have control over market process and thus can be held responsible for market outcomes. According to social Darwinists, those who fail in market competition do not have a right to demand compensation from those who succeed.

But one wonders why we should go to such lengths to justify economic freedom when we can argue that economic freedom is an essential individual right. If economic freedom is a basic individual right, we can say that economic freedom is good as an end in itself because it protects and enhances the dignity and worth of the individual person. To Milton Friedman, economic freedom is as important as civil liberties because the former is as a guardian of the latter.

Whatever the moral justifications, we have to devise ways to secure and protect individual economic freedom if we accept its vital role in a market economy. Like political rights, economic rights must be embedded in the system of the rule of law.

Economists have long emphasized the importance of the rule of law in economic development (North 1989). Without certain rules of the game regulating the uncertainty and opportunistic behavior inherent in actual market conditions, market economies cannot function effectively because there would be too many opportunities for mutually beneficial transactions. What kind of rules does a market economy need?

Qian (2000) offers two main functions of law in a market economy. "First, the rule of law regulates and limits discretionary interventions of the state in economic activities. Second, the rule of law regulates the economic behavior of individuals and enterprises to create an orderly, stable environment with fair competition, clearly defined and well-protected property rights, and effectively enforced contracts. In essence, these two economic functions of the rule of law are about regulating the relationship between the state and the market through legal institutions so that economic development is both possible and sustainable."

Qian's argument implies that there are two main threats to individual rights, government and "badly behaving" private actors, and the rule of law is necessary to protect individual economic rights from both of them. There are countless examples of the state violating individual property rights, the most direct case of which is nationalization of industries. More subtle examples include discretionary bureaucratic actions restricting individuals' ownership rights and informal government pressures to make sacrifices in the name of public good (such as bailing out failed companies).

Violations of property rights may be more common in the private realm even though their magnitude may not be as large. Failure to carry out one's contractual duty seems to be the most common form of property rights violation. The problems of unaccountable corporate managers and malefactors of securities law also fall into this category. Extreme examples exist in the private sector, for example, organized crime using violence to take away other people's property.

The concept of individual economic rights is not limited to a defensive right to protect one's physical or intangible assets. One can argue that a chance to compete fairly is also an individual economic right. Then the rule of law should ensure that neither the government nor private actors engage in practices undermining fair market competition.

To summarize, a market economy is a system based on individual rights, and the rule of law regulating the relationships among economic agents in a market economy is designed first and foremost to protect and enhance individual economic rights. Seen this way, the priorities of market reform become clear. The main focus of market reform efforts should be on the safeguarding of individual economic rights, rather than on market outcomes such as efficiency, competition, or deregulation that are generally expected to follow from the presence of strong individual rights.

## Korean Market Economy and the Rule of Law

The Korean economy since the 1960s poses a puzzle. On the one hand, it has been a successful example of market reform—Korea and Taiwan were the first among developing countries to let their industries compete in world markets. On the other hand, the Korean economy until the economic crisis had been touted as an example of a nonfree market model of economic development. Only in the midst of an economic crisis in the late 1990s, was an intellectual consensus formed in support of building a genuine market economy in Korea.

The old Korean model of economic development was not based on a market economy; simply, the government allocated credit to favored sectors through policy loans and administrative guidance (Cho and Kim 1995). Since it was the government that decided where the money went, the banks did not really have an incentive to develop their own capacity for project evaluation. Moreover, risks for the banks were minimal because the government provided explicit guarantees for depositors while it bailed out the companies that they supported. The government thus acted as an "effective risk partner" of private industry.

This implicit co-insurance scheme among government, banks, and industry worked well for a long time, fueling the industrialization of the Korean economy. As its limitations began to show in the early 1980s, however, the Korean government began seeking to reform the old model. The very same policies that were once hailed as effective means for socialization of risk were increasingly seen as sources of macroeconomic stability, moral hazard, and crony capitalism.

President Chun Doo Hwan attempted to change the 1970s legacy of high inflation and government intervention, first with macroeconomic stabilization and later with a program of deregulation and liberalization. During this period, the government ended formal, open, and selective promotions of industries by replacing all industry-specific promotion acts with one sector-neutral industry promotion act in 1986. The Chun government also initiated a voluntary program of financial deregulation and liberalization. The focus of reform shifted to social welfare and economic justice when the democratic reforms of 1986 and 1987 unleashed reform demands from previously disadvantaged sectors, such as agriculture and small- and medium-sized enterprises.

These efforts, however, had not significantly changed the old Korean model, and the Korean economy paid a high price for this failure with the economic crisis of 1997. The 1997 crisis stemmed from the same structural problems that the Korean government had been trying to tackle since the early 1980s, namely, mismanaged banks, government intervention in credit allocation, highly leveraged chaebol, and rigid labor markets. Reflecting these concerns, the agreement between the Korean government and the International Monetary Fund provided for specific reform measures covering all three areas. To facilitate corporate restructuring and improve labor market flexibility, the Korean government promised to make it easier for firms to lay off workers. The government also committed itself to accelerating ongoing programs of deregulation and liberalization, restructuring financial institutions, enhancing transparency in financial transactions, and strengthening prudential regulation and supervision. At the same time, the government agreed to make the chaebol more transparent and accountable by forcing them to report combined financial statements and to discontinue mutual-payment guarantees in which chaebol parent companies promised to pay third-party lenders if their member firms defaulted.

Where is the Korean economy now? Although Korea made progress on the restructuring of its heavily indebted corporate and financial sectors, it is unclear whether the basic rules of the game changed in any fundamental way. Critics would first point to the problems of a weak legal system. The rule of law does not seem to be working anywhere, whether in the corporate, labor or financial sector.

One reason for the slow progress toward a market economy is that Korea has not approached the problem of economic reform from the point of view of individual rights. We can see this in at least three ways. First, the Korean government is not yet fully committed to the protection of individual rights. The government routinely violates the property rights of individuals and enterprises. Many real estate regulations impose such extreme restrictions on buying and selling that exercising property rights is virtually impossible. Nor does the government regulate private business practices that impinge on individual property rights and the ability to compete fairly. Protecting small shareholders from managers is one area in which the government could have been inactive. Pervasive unfair business practices also stymie fair competition in many areas.

Second, the government has been more willing to compromise the principles of individual rights and the rule of law in an effort to achieve certain reform outcomes (Mo and Moon 1999). When implementing economic reforms, the Kim Dae Jung government used informal administrative guidance with an implicit threat of sanctions. In carrying out financial reform, for example, the government dictated the terms of restructuring to private financial institutions, and some of its decisions, such as bank closings, were viewed as arbitrary and politically motivated. As a result, bank shareholders and employees protested, sometimes violently, the government's restructuring plan.

In corporate reform, too, the rule of law has been compromised in favor of administrative guidance. The government used its control of banks to force the chaebol to improve their financial structure and streamline their business activities. Banks had enormous power over the chaebol as their main creditors, they could practically bankrupt firms by cutting off credit. Among the measures that the government has tried to implement through the banks so far, the reduction of debt ratios and "big deals" has been most controversial. Regardless of their economic logic, these measures raised serious concerns about the rule of law and thus about democratic principles and President Kim's confidence in market mechanisms. Bank-led corporate restructuring is a case in point. Admittedly, the banks had some role to play in the management of the firms to which they lent. However, it was not appropriate for the banks to force their debtors to give up business lines and reduce debt ratios when the debtors were not formally in default. It is especially troublesome because the chaebol, upon receiving such demands from their main creditor bank, could not turn to another bank. No bank was in a position to do business against the wishes of the government.

Third, reform rhetoric has been overly collectivist. The government always tries to justify economic reforms in terms of public good. A market economy has been promoted not as a means to realize the full potential of individual ability or to enhance the dignity and worth of the individual, but as a tool to promote national economic interests. There is no doubt that the government has to appeal to national interests. But Korea is certainly unusual in the lack of attention that the public debate on economic reform pays to the need for protecting individual rights.

Disregard for the sanctity of individual rights has serious consequences. When individual economic actors see their rights violated in the name of public good, they do not feel "ownership" of economic reforms. They see the reforms serving the political interests of those in power and their political allies. If this perception is pervasive, the economic reforms are not sustainable because when there is a change of power, the new government would not continue them or the public does not try to stop the new government from reneging on the commitments of the old government. In order to make economic reforms sustainable, therefore, enough individuals have to feel it is in their interest to support them. There is no better way to achieve this than to concentrate on basic economic rights available to all individuals and enterprises.

## What Should Be Done?

Promoting the rule of law is a difficult exercise both in theory and practice (Carothers 2003). There is not enough accumulated knowledge on the development of the rule of law to know with confidence which reforms will work and which will not. But in the East Asian context, a more vigorous debate is likely to have a positive impact because it is clear that not enough attention has been paid to the importance of the sanctity of the individual person in the rule of law debate.

Given this shortcoming, the first task for legal reform in East Asia must be promoting better understanding of and education on the importance of the individual person. First, the public must understand that the basic function of the rule of law is to protect their individual rights. Too many people believe that the law exists to combat or punish the bad or serve the interests of the ruling class. It is a common saying in Korea that a good man is "one who can live without the law."

Second, the fact that individuals have certain inalienable rights that even a legitimately elected government cannot violate should be part of everyone's moral code. Too often, it is buried underneath public consciousness in frequent outbursts of collectivist sentiments. Although the society can restrict individual rights in certain situations, it should be an exception, not a rule.

Third, it is the individual citizen, not just the government, on whom the responsibility for upholding the rule of law falls. In this regard, it is important for individual citizens to be more active in protecting their rights and furthering their interests through private enforcement. There is a limit to what individual citizens can achieve through public law.

But realistically, education alone is not going to be sufficient. Leaders must exhibit exemplary behavior or voluntary public compliance cannot be expected. The role of leaders is particularly important in East Asia because their "arrogant" attitude toward the rule of law, that is, their belief that they stand above the law, has been often cited as the factor most detrimental to the rule of law.

History also shows that leaders can make a difference (Widner 2005). "Effective leaders can not only implement new [reform measures], but also can change public opinion and, over time, the nature of legal practice itself." Two examples come to mind. The first is King John, when he agreed to the Magna Carta in 1215. The second is the roles of Chief Justice John Marshall and President Thomas Jefferson in establishing the judicial review of legislative and executive actions in the case of Marbury vs. Madison in 1803. What these successful legal reformers had in common were a deep conviction in principles, personal moderation, and example and respect for individual autonomy. More than ever, East Asia needs such leadership from its political leaders to move forward toward the rule of law.

## The Korean Rule of Law by Issue and Sector

While understanding and addressing the problem of the rule of law at the national level, it is important to recognize that debates on the rule of law in Korea are taking place issue by issue and sector by sector. The primary purpose of this volume is to gain a broad understanding of the rule of law in Korea by examining each of its major issues separately. Contributors to this volume show that the rule of law in Korea is a work in progress; they report significant progress toward a rule-based system in their issue areas, and they identify a number of problems retarding that progress.

In his chapter on the current debate in Korea over the need for changing the constitution, former Justice of the Supreme Court Lee Hoi-Chang, who later also served as Korea's prime minister, makes the case for not tampering with the constitution at this juncture. Drawing on his unique experience as both a judge and a politician, he presents a personal, yet balanced and dispassionate argument for resisting the temptation to revise the constitution. For Lee, there are two types of change being put forward by advocates of a constitutional revision. One is based on the argument that there are certain gaps or shortcomings in the current constitution and that these need to be filled in or rectified through an amendment. The other type is much more broad-based—it calls for a total redrafting of the constitution so as to create a more perfect constitution better suited for the 21st century.

After reviewing the various arguments for change and the alleged defects in the current constitution on which the arguments are based, Lee concludes that all can be opposed with counterarguments and counterexamples and that the proposed amendments might even create new problems. Moreover, he concludes, these complaints about constitutional defects are essentially based on perceived inconvenience of the current system, none of which amounts to a persuasive and urgent need for changing the constitution. With regard to the more open-ended arguments for totally revamping the constitution, Lee cautions that such an approach could provide occasion for undermining the constitution's core values such as protection of individual rights, a liberal democracy, and a market economy. More important, he warns against the "fatal conceit" that a perfect constitution could be made through utopian social engineering. Lee concludes the chapter with a reminder that while the politicians are embroiled in the debate over constitutional revision, Korea's standing in the international political and economic arena has been steadily falling.

The chapter by Hahm Chaihark is an analysis of a number of recent significant developments in Korea relating to the rule of law at the constitutional level. For Hahm, these developments can be seen as different milestones on Korea's sometimes-rocky path toward finding a proper balance between constitutionalism and democracy. In the first part of the chapter, which briefly reviews the process by which the Constitutional Court emerged as an important player in a post-1987 context, the author suggests that the court's popularity as a champion of individual rights and democratic reform may be coming to an end as it starts to deal less with transitional issues and more with laws passed by legislatures with more democratic legitimacy. The court has reached a juncture at which it needs to think hard about its role if it wishes to continue to enjoy positive public esteem.

In the second part of the chapter, Hahm presents an analysis of a few high-profile cases decided by the Constitutional Court within the past few years with a view to finding some intimations on the direction in which the court intends to chart its future course. The three cases described all seem to suggest that the court is taking on an increasingly assertive role in "guarding" the constitution as the final arbiter of constitutional meaning—even as against democratically elected presidents and legislatures. Whether that will result in a "juristocracy," only time will tell. And finally, as the author describes in the third part of the chapter, there are forces currently afoot in Korea that tend to pull in the other direction. These include increasing demands for more democratic input on judicial appointments to the nation's highest courts and for more democratic participation in the administration of justice, in the form of juries and/or lay judges. These are certainly trends that need to be taken into account if the Constitutional Court indeed has ambitions of becoming the "guardian of the constitution."

In chapter three, "The Two Tales of the South Korean Presidency: Imperial But Imperiled Presidency," Hoon Jaung argues that the South Korean presidency has become a Janus-faced executive, which in turn calls for further institutional and political reform toward a better practice of rule of law. Jaung discusses how even though the president has been subject to enhanced checks on his power, he still sustains many features of a traditional imperial president. Specifically, the president is an imperial president for the first 18 months of his tenure, whereafter he becomes a lame-duck president.

The lack of, or limited growth of, vertical and horizontal accountability is responsible for sustaining an imperial president, a legacy from the authoritarian era, during the early phase of the five-year tenure. Both the National Assembly and political parties still exert only limited restraints on the presidential power due to a dearth of resources, expertise, and information. Jaung points out that although democratic transition has enhanced the institutional legitimacy of the National Assembly, the legislative branch is not highly effective in constraining the power of the president. The public has also failed in putting pressure on presidential power during the early phase of presidential tenure. As the South Korean public tends to give enthusiastic support for the newly elected president during the first year, the president is poorly restrained. Then the president shifts from imperial president to imperiled president after his first year in office. Several factors are responsible for this remarkable change in presidential power. First, the nonconcurrent electoral cycle is responsible for the fall of presidential influence on his party. Second, the gradual decline of public approval contributes to enfeebling the president. In a word, for South Korea to have a strong but restrained president, South Korean democracy needs reforms in the electoral cycle and presidential tenure and more enhanced checks from the National Assembly and political parties.

Jongryn Mo in chapter four addresses the persistent problem of campaign finance corruption in Korean politics. The good news is that the role of money in Korean presidential politics has been declining since democratization began in 1987. The amounts of money that the ruling party has been able to raise have decreased, and more important, there is evidence that the share of illegal contributions has also fallen. The bad news is that this improvement in the rule of law in campaign financing has come largely from increased party competition—which tends to lower the bargaining power of political parties with respect to their donors—not from stronger enforcement of the laws. As a result, the Korean system of presidential campaign finance may not be able to guard itself from the potential forces of grand corruption if the level of political competition significantly decreases in the future.

The rule of law still remains elusive in Korean corporate governance in terms of effectively minimizing agency costs associated with controlling shareholders. Joongi Kim in chapter five explores what has hindered the establishment of rule of law in corporate governance. Rule of law will be assessed ultimately through the effective operation of and compliance with the laws associated with corporate governance. This chapter first describes the corporate governance environment prior to the financial crisis. It argues that the postauthoritarian legacy, in which the state actively intervened in the economic realm, still lingers. The inability to develop an effective infrastructure based upon hard law can be attributed to past overreliance on soft laws and controls.

The chapter then describes the emergence of rule of law in terms of corporate governance in the post-crisis period. It discusses how the governance of corporations has been influenced in terms of the rule of law as it relates to hard law, soft law, and market practices. Various court cases are examined to show what needs to be done to improve the rule of law in corporate governance. In the end, to evolve toward a liberal market economy, effective rule of law in the form of market-based checks and balances must be established. An efficient and disciplined market-based economy would also help prevent the reoccurrence of such devastation as financial contagion. The author concludes that Korea's corporate governance has made an important transition toward the establishment of rule of law.

As the political and economic side effects of "governing the market" became clear by the end of the 1980s, "the rule of law" became an increasingly relevant concept in Korea. One of the most significant developments in this regard was the enactment of the Monopoly Regulation and Fair Trade Act in 1980. Previous efforts to introduce competition law had failed because eliminating entry barriers and promoting competition would have gone against the government-managed economic system.

After the limitations of the government-managed economy became clear in the aftermath of the heavy and chemical industry drive, however, the government began to embrace genuine competition policy. Wonhyuk Lim explains in chapter six that this shift in emphasis from industrial policy to competition policy was a precursor to a more fundamental transition from a developmental authoritarianism to a democratic market economy in Korea.

Property rights in Korea have not been firmly institutionalized because Korea has insufficient institutions to delineate and protect private property. Worse, the rule of politics has more influence than the rule of law when an economic player exercises recognized property rights. In particular, large conglomerates (chaebol) have grown rapidly in Korea, and with the idea of stakeholder capitalism prevailing, disputes over property rights of conglomerates have been on the rise.

Sang-young Rhyu examines this problem with a case study of the Samsung Life initial public offering (IPO), an institutional process that delineates and distributes property rights in a firm. Samsung Life Insurance did not give up its tendency to rely on the rule of politics rather than the rule of law. The company has decided to remain at its status quo. In other words, the objection of Samsung Life Insurance to its IPO means that it would not redelineate its corporate property rights in legal terms and divide or distribute property rights under the current circumstances in which disputes concerning property rights arose. Of course, the government, including the Financial Supervisory Commission, opted for political compromise and decided to remain at its status quo. In this regard, when the government prefers political compromise and the rule of politics, the state is not necessarily the most efficient protector against all aspects of theft. How can property rights be free from the effect of politics and be institutionalized? The capitalism of Korea will be upgraded by one step only when property rights are institutionalized and democracy is consolidated by strengthening the rule of law and sustaining the development of the market economy.

## References

Carothers, Thomas. 2003. "Promoting the Rule of Law Abroad: The Problem of Knowledge." Working Paper, Carnegie Endowment for International Peace.

Hager, Barry. 2000. *The Rule of Law: A Lexicon for Policymakers.* Mansfield Center for Pacific Affairs.

Hahm, Pyong Choon. 1986. *Korean Jurisprudence, Politics, and Culture*. Yonsei University Press.

Hofstede, Geert. 1991. *Cultures and Organizations*. New York: McGraw Hill.

Kang, Jung In. 2003. "The Rule of Law and the Rule of Virtue: On the Necessity for Their Mutual Integration." *Korea Journal* (spring).

Mo, Jongryn and Chung-in Moon. 1999. "Korea after the Crash." *Journal of Democracy*, 10: 150–164.

North, Douglass. 1999. "Institutions and Economic Growth: A Historical Introduction." In *International Political Economy*, eds. Jeffrey Frieden and David Lake.

Park, Dongsuh and Kwangwoong Kim. 1987. *Korean Attitude Toward Democracy*. Seoul National University Press (in Korean).

Pei, Minxin. "China's Governance Crisis." *Foreign Affairs*. September/October 2002

Qian, Yinqyi. 2000. "The Modern Market Economy and the Rule of Law." *Perspectives*, volume 1, number 5.

Widner, Jennifer. 2005. "Reflections on Judicial Reform." Working Paper, Department of Political Science, University of Michigan.

# CHAPTER ONE

# The Constitution Should Not Be Tampered With

## Lee Hoi-Chang

## Introduction

Arguments for revising the Korean constitution seem to be taking on momentum these days. A number of prime ministers of the Roh Moo Hyun administration first intoned the need for a constitutional revision. They were followed by the Speaker of the National Assembly, whose first public statement was a proposal to revise the constitution so as to make it more fit for the 21st century. Discussions on constitutional revision are also spreading fast among constitutional scholars and specialists.

Roughly speaking, arguments for revising the constitution can be divided into two positions. One claims that the current constitution is inconvenient or deficient in some of its parts and therefore needs to be supplemented. The other camp claims that what is needed is to draft an entirely new and more perfect constitution better suited for the 21st century.

The Korean constitution, however, is a "rigid constitution" in the sense that the procedures for its revision have been made intentionally more difficult than in the case of ordinary laws. A proposal for a revision must be passed by a vote of at least two-thirds of the members of the National Assembly, then it must be ratified by a national referendum in which it must be supported by at least half of all votes cast by at least half of all voters eligible to vote in a general election.

This is intended to ensure that the constitution will be revised only with the utmost circumspection. As such, the argument for revision based on mere inconvenience or partial deficiency is, I think, misguided.

Regarding the argument for total revision based on the alleged need for a new and future-oriented constitution, I think this too is without merit. As I shall show below, the very idea of an ideal constitution better suited for the 21st century has no substance or practicality. Moreover, it is my belief that the proper time for a total revision should be when we are at the stage of preparing a new constitution for a unified Korea.

Although there may be points worth listening to in the discussions among constitutional scholars and experts, the arguments originating from the politicians seem mostly intended to enhance their own sectarian interests. We need to guard against constitutional revisions being used as a tool for interest group politics. Here, I shall survey the major reasons put forth by people calling for a constitutional revision as well as the counterarguments that may be made in response.

## Why Should the Constitution Be Revised?

The major points presented as grounds for a constitutional revision follow. Before I proceed any further, however, I should make it clear that I am neither a scholar nor an expert on this matter, and what I present here is not meant to be a scholarly or expert opinion. These are just my candid thoughts on the recent discussions on constitutional revision, from the perspective of someone who has had a chance to participate, as a justice of the supreme court and as a prime minister, in the actual operations of the government and to experience, as the leader of the opposition and as a presidential candidate, the political realities surrounding the relationship between the president and the National Assembly.

## Allowing the President to Seek Reelection

On the relative strengths and weaknesses of a single-term presidency as against a system that allows reelection, much was discussed during the last constitutional revision in 1987. My recollection is that at the time, the single-term presidency was preferred out of a critical response to a system that allowed a second term.

Interestingly, recent advocates of constitutional revision are now criticizing the single-term presidency for encouraging short-term policy objectives due to the fact that longer-term objectives are not realizable within the incumbent's term of office; for promoting an early lame-duck situation due to the fact that the there is no chance for the incumbent to be in power long; and for eroding democratic accountability because the people have no chance to pass judgment on the incumbent's performance.

First of all, the point about single-term presidency causing undue focus on short-term policies is not as serious as one might expect. The fact is that during the term of past several presidents, all of whom were in office for a single term, many important long-term projects at the national level were formulated and are still being implemented. (Examples include projects on the high-speed railway system and the new airport in Incheon during the Roh Tae Woo administration, and restructuring the agricultural production system and constructing the information superhighway during the Kim Young Sam administration.) By contrast, a system that allows a second term may actually encourage short-term projects as the incumbent will wish to attain some "achievements" during the first term that will help him get reelected.

Also, the point about single-term presidency causing early lame-duck phenomena is considerably exaggerated. As a general matter, any president who has just been elected enjoys a high approval rating at the beginning of his term, which allows him to exercise great powers. Right after their inaugurations, Presidents Kim Dae Jung and Kim

Young Sam's approval ratings were 87 percent and 81 percent, respectively. Typically, an incumbent president becomes a lame duck
when there is about a year or so left in his term. Thus, a president
facing a few difficulties at the beginning of his administration or politicians being embroiled in some conflicts should not be mistaken as
a sign of a lame-duck presidency. By contrast, it has been reported
that under a system that allows reelection, the president is likely to
become a lame duck from the very beginning of the second term.
President Roh Moo Hyun's troubles in the management of state affairs, which started from very early on in his term, should not be
regarded as a lame-duck phenomenon caused by the single-term system; rather, the president's difficulties are a result of ineptitude and
lack of experience on the part of his administration.

Next, the argument that democratic accountability is undermined
because the people are deprived of a chance to pass judgment on the
incumbent's performance is also weak and unpersuasive. If that were
true, we would still face the same problem under a two-term system
if an incumbent chose not to seek reelection or if the president had
already served a second term. Since neither of them would be sub-
jected to the people's judgment, we would have to conclude that a
two-term system likewise undermines democratic accountability.
Moreover, even under a single-term presidency, the people do have
the ability to express their approval of the president at the next presidential election through their votes toward the candidate from the
president's party and at the general and local elections held during
the president's term. The results of the 1997 presidential election
held in the midst of the Asian financial crisis and the local elections
held on May 31, 2006, are good examples.

In fact, a system that allows reelection has some flaws not found
in a single-term system. As the president's first priority will be to
secure reelection, during the first term it is highly likely that he will
concentrate on implementing policies designed to curry favor with
the people so as to win their votes. Further, a president running for

reelection will no doubt be in a much more advantageous position than the opposition candidate, which is problematic in terms of fairness and impartiality of the election.

Advocates of constitutional revision also claim that under the current five-year single-term system elections are too frequent because the terms for the president and members of the National Assembly are different and that this mismatch is likely to result in a so-called divided government in which the ruling party holds minority seats in the National Assembly. Therefore, they argue, a four-year two-term system is needed so as to synchronize the election terms. It is certainly true that different electoral terms mean that elections come around very often, and it may indeed be more convenient to synchronize them. Yet does this amount to a defect that has to be corrected immediately through a constitutional revision?

First of all, presidential elections and general elections for the members of the National Assembly have completely different meanings, both of which must be respected. If the two elections are held simultaneously, however, it is very probable that one will receive relatively less attention. Candidates in the general election may be too occupied with their own campaigns, and thus the presidential race will be determined by the individual personality or image of the candidates, turning it into a popularity contest. On the other hand, the general elections may be overshadowed by national issues that determine the presidential elections, in which case local issues will not receive the proper consideration. On the issue of divided government, I shall have more to say later.

In light of the preceding, it may be difficult to say with certainty which is better, a single-term presidency or a system that allows re-election, but I am convinced that at present there is no logically superior and urgent reason for a constitutional change toward a two-term system. If anything, given the possibility which I will show below that even a partial revision such as this may trigger a more fundamental discussion on the basic principles and identity of the constitution, I believe that it is improper to broach the topic of revision at all.

## Abolishing Prime Ministership and Creating the Position of Vice President

Some argue for the elimination of the position of prime minister based on the rationale that this system promotes confrontation and discord in the government because the president tends to regard the prime minister as the head of the administration while seeing himself as the head of state, which causes him to view criticism from the legislature or opposition party as selfish, politically motivated obstructions thrown at his attempt to implement a supposedly higher vision for the whole nation that transcends the political divide. In other words, the existence of the prime minister tends to cause the president to be either dismissive of or confrontational toward such criticism, thereby undermining the government's capacity for dialogue and conciliation.

It is true that past presidents have regarded themselves as the head of state rather than the head of administration and tended to assume an imperious attitude in their management of state affairs, with no room for negotiation or compromise, which only intensified conflict and friction. It is incorrect, however, to attribute this to the system of prime ministership. The cause should rather be found in the past presidents' failure to understand the status of the president under a government of separation of powers. Even with no prime minister, they still would have regarded themselves as heads of state rather than heads of administration, and acted as if they were superior to the legislative or judicial branches of the government.

Do we then really need the position of prime minister? According to the constitution, the prime minister is to aid the president and to direct the various ministries of the government. In reality, however, past presidents were in direct control of both domestic and foreign affairs, thinking that the role of the prime minister and other ministers was merely one of assisting them and faithfully implementing their will. Thus, the prime minister's role was often limited to being an "on-behalf-of" prime minister[1] or a "cannon-fodder" prime minister.

Yet this was based on a misunderstanding of the institution of the prime ministership. It is practically impossible for the president to personally manage every aspect of the affairs of the state. That is why the constitution gives the prime minister the power to direct the various ministries, so as to allow him to have a role in the governance of the state. In this connection, the expression "Prime Minister Responsibility System" used by some is inappropriate. According to the constitution, the prime minister is an assistant to the president and therefore even if he had a role in administering the affairs of the state, he is not constitutionally responsible to the people or the National Assembly.

The prime minister's power to direct the ministries is truly important as a means for ensuring consistency and continuity over time in the policies formulated and implemented by the various ministries as well as for coordinating the interests and operations of those ministries. The president, for his part, must respect the prime minister's power over the ministries and should establish a tradition of always going through the prime minister when dealing with the individual ministries. If the president or the Blue House were to call on each of the ministers personally and get involved with their daily operations, the ministries will start competing for the president's favor and there will no longer be any consistency or cooperation among the ministries. As a result, the president and the Blue House will be faced with a burden too heavy to handle.

When I served as prime minister in the Kim Young Sam administration, I strongly urged the president to put this into practice, but

1. [Translator's note] The reference is to the practice of having Prime Minister read the President's speeches at public functions, which the Prime Minister would invariably end with the phase "read by so-and-so on behalf of the President."

I was refused. Eventually, I resigned from the position due to increasing conflict with President Kim over my attempt to implement this understanding of the prime minister's role. As far as I know, President Roh Moo Hyun is the first to pledge a significant role for the Prime Minister and to actually practice some kind of division of labor between the prime minister and the president. Although his efforts came to naught due to the overbearing and arrogant actions of then–Prime Minister Lee Hae Chan, President Roh's attempt to implement a division of labor deserves recognition.

Next, the argument for creating the position of vice president in lieu of that of prime minister is based on the supposed benefit that derives from having the vice president perform emergency duties in case the president becomes incapacitated as well as the possibility of power-sharing and of having the views of certain minorities or regions represented in the government. According to the current constitution, however, the prime minister is authorized to be the acting president during the president's incapacity, and since this arrangement is a temporary measure expected to last for only a short period of time, I see no serious problem posed by the prime minister's acting as the president. In fact, back in 2004, we actually saw Prime Minister Goh Kun assume the powers of the presidency for a short time when President Roh Moo Hyun's powers were suspended as a result of the National Assembly's decision to impeach him.

As for the alleged benefits of power-sharing with the president, I believe the current system of division of labor between the prime minister and the president is a more realistic and workable arrangement. Historically, there were cases, under President Syngman Rhee's government, in which the vice presidency was used to satisfy the interests of minorities and regions. But Vice President Yi Si Young and Vice President Kim Sung Soo all resigned because of their clashes with the mainstream faction in the government. These examples lead me to be skeptical of the arguments for creating the position of vice president.

Some advocates of the vice presidency argue that in Korea, where parties are highly cohesive and hierarchical, running mates from the same faction or at least similar factions will not be prone to such power struggles. Yet if both the president and the vice president are from the same political faction, what would be the point of adopting the system of vice president? Furthermore, the argument is based on flawed assumptions, because nowadays, Korean political parties are showing less and less cohesiveness internally and are becoming much less hierarchical than in the past.

## On the So-Called Problem of Divided Government

Advocates of constitutional revision claim that the current system encourages the emergence of governments in which the party of the president is the minority party in the legislature, that is, a divided government. They argue that due to the different electoral cycles, there is little room for the president's popularity to have any impact on the general elections and that, if anything, a desire to check the president's activity is likely to be stronger, which will result in giving majority seats to the opposition parties. They further point out that under such a divided government, the effectiveness of government administration will inevitably suffer.

Yet this is not necessarily so. Even when the election periods are not synchronized, if the president's approval rate is very high, this may well translate into the people's willingness to support him in carrying out his policies and to elect a legislature in which the president's party is in the majority. By contrast, even if the president's approval rate is very high, when the ruling party and its legislators are out of favor with the people, the electorate's decision in the presidential election may well be segregated and independent from their decisions when choosing their representatives in the National Assembly. This will be so even if the two elections are held at the same time. In other words, the argument that the unsynchronized elections contribute to the formation of a divided government is based on faulty reasoning, as the exact opposite scenario may be just as possible.

The argument that divided governments will lower the governance capability or effectiveness of the government puzzles and bewilders me. To be sure, in a unified government in which the president's party is the majority party, the legislature will more likely move according to the will of the president, and the government will probably have more governance capability or effectiveness. Yet is it not the case that past presidents of Korea have tended to be "imperial" presidents who wielded too much power concentrated on their person? And was this not the reason our goal for the past few years has been consistently to diffuse and check the powers of the president? Seen from this angle, to take issue with the fact that the legislature's ability to check the president's powers has been enhanced, saying that this is lowering the competence of the government, is to fundamentally misunderstand the most basic principles of separation of powers and checks and balances. It is also to ignore the recent memories of our efforts to prevent such imperial presidents from exercising so much power.

Short of switching to a parliamentary cabinet system, a divided government will be both a constant possibility and a natural phenomenon under a presidential system (and even under a semi-presidential system). Therefore, instead of complaining about the possibility of a divided government, the ruling party should make more of an effort to ensure that they obtain majority seats in the legislature. Also, instead of relying on such underhanded measures as luring away opposition legislators to cross the aisle and change their party affiliations, the president when faced with a divided government should concentrate on more legitimate ways of enhancing the effectiveness of the government. These would be to apply his democratic statesmanship skills and demonstrating a leadership of unity based on active persuasion. This means regarding the opposition party as a legitimate partner in state governance, to be conferred with and to cooperate with on a regular basis. This means personally seeking out opposition members, when needed, to win them over. That is what democratic statesmanship and leadership of unity is all about.

In the United States, which also has a presidential system, a divided government can be seen regularly. A recent example would be the Clinton administration, which had to work with a Congress dominated by the opposing party. Nevertheless, I have yet to hear of anybody arguing for a constitutional amendment to prevent such situations from arising again, nor even of anyone regarding it as a problem to be fixed. In fact, these are times when the president is able to truly show his leadership abilities.

Some argue that such leadership of persuasion and "seeking the common ground" can work only in countries like the United States where party discipline is weak and decentralized, whereas in countries like Korea the parties are much more collectivistic and have centralized structures. My sense, however, is that Korean political parties, particularly opposition parties, are becoming increasingly less collectivistic and less hierarchical, with party discipline getting weaker and negotiation groups taking more important roles, so individual lawmakers are much freer to express their own views.

As a leader of the opposition party during Kim Dae Jung's presidency, I had a chance to experience personally a divided government. At the time, the Kim Dae Jung administration did complain about the fact that they were a minority government, but what lowered the government's effectiveness was not the opposition's being the majority party, but rather it was the useless internal conflict within the so-called coalition government between the president's party and the United Liberal Democrats over an alleged promise to change to a parliamentary system.

As the opposition party at the time, the Grand National Party maintained the position of cooperating with the government on issues relating to the economy and the people's livelihood while strongly criticizing and restraining the government on issues of the inter-Korean relationship, for we believed that the Kim administration's policy toward North Korea was endangering our national security. Indeed, the government's policy of unilateral assistance for North Korea, based as it is on a complete disregard for principles of reciprocity and transparency, has brought about this precarious situation in which the North is threatening the peace in Northeast Asia—and the world—with its nuclear weapons and ballistic missiles.

From my past experiences, I am convinced that although a divided government may reduce the effectiveness of the government, this is not due to any resistance from the legislature or the opposition, but is because the president and the government failed to work with the opposition earnestly and failed to show leadership of unity based on the art of persuasion.

President Roh Moo Hyun once expressed his frustration at being a minority government by referring to himself as a "vegetable president." Of course this may be a challenging situation for the president, but it should be recalled that it was Prime Minister Lee Hae Chan who damaged the relationship with the opposition horribly by appearing at the National Assembly and showing nothing but contempt and arrogance toward opposition lawmakers. In sum, the difficulties that the current administration has experienced is due less to a legislature of the opposition party and more to the utter lack of democratic statesmanship ability or any will to work with the opposition through negotiation and compromise.

## On Parliamentarism and Semi-Presidentialism

We all know that presidentialism and parliamentarism have their relative strengths and weaknesses, so I shall not go into them here. I would just like to examine the issues of representativeness and accountability, which are often offered as grounds for the alleged need to change the current presidential system to a parliamentary one.

The argument is that a president must perform two potentially conflicting roles simultaneously—the nonpartisan role of representing the whole nation and uniting the people and the decidedly partisan role of leading the ruling party in the political contest against the opposition party. If the president concentrates on his nonpartisan role as the head of state, then his status as the people's representative and his accountability will suffer, because both are acquired through his party affiliation. If, on the other hand, he focuses on his role as the leader of his party and engages in conflicts with the opposition, then he will only encourage contention among people rather than uniting the nation. In order to avoid this dilemma, say some, we need to revise the constitution to adopt either a parliamentary or semi-presidential system.

I believe this is a very formalistic argument that fails to take into account the reality. A prime minister under a parliamentary system is required, no less than the president is, to exhibit leadership to unite the people and represent the nation. The president must, on the other hand, actively persuade the opposition party on policies of his administration through negotiation and compromise while averting a political deadlock by influencing his own party to retract or alter policies and bills that he thinks will lead to extreme partisan discord. These are roles that any head of government must play, and it makes no difference whether it is a president or a parliament. In other words, even if the government party and the opposition have reached an impasse and are unable to compromise, it has no bearing on the president's status as the people's representative.

There are, of course, other reasons offered by scholars and other experts in support of the parliamentary system, and they all deserve our consideration, but despite all the strengths of that system, I do not think they are strong enough to convince us that it is actually better suited to the Korean context than presidentialism. Even though each has its own merits and demerits, presidentialism, in my view, is the better choice given that—unlike members of a parliament and political parties, which cannot help but be influenced by each electoral district's mood and lobbying—the president is at least able to

make policies and set the course for the whole nation based on national interests and the benefit of the people without being swayed
by partisan opinions and pressure groups. To be sure, a president may
be held hostage to populism or some extreme political ideology and
cause a major disorder or endanger the state, but that is a factor of
the individual president's qualities and not a problem inherent in the
presidential system itself.

Regarding the so-called semi-presidential system, it is essentially
a product of a compromise between presidentialism and parliamentarism. Therefore, it may have the strengths of both systems, but it
may also exhibit the weaknesses of both. Based on the experience of
France, which has a semi-presidential system, many commentators
have observed that when the president's party has the majority in the
legislature, the government becomes even more centralized under a
strong, dominant president, and when the president's party is in the
minority, then a so-called co-habitation government is born in which
the potential for clash between the president and the legislature becomes even greater than under a presidential system. I see no need
to change to a semi-presidential system.

## A Constitution Should Not Be Tampered With Lightly

I have surveyed the major arguments of the advocates of constitutional revision and offered my rebuttals. This was not so much to
prove the absolute superiority of any particular position, but rather to
show that all of the arguments offered in favor of a revision may be
opposed with a counterargument. Further, I wanted to raise the question whether, despite the contestability of these arguments, we are
faced with such an urgent situation as to require a constitutional
revision.

A constitution is the fundamental law of a state. As such, it embodies the principle values of the state and is a reflection of its identity, in addition to being a framework for the protection of the basic
rights of the citizens and the government structure. Since it is the

fundamental law, a constitution must be respected. Unlike ordinary laws, it should not be tampered with just because it is partially inconvenient or incomplete. Rather, it should gradually be made as complete as possible, through interpretation that will bring the constitution in step with the changing times.

Less-developed countries tend to change their constitutions often. This tends to foster a contemptuous attitude toward the constitution and eventually destabilizes the constitutional order. In Korea, the first constitution was established in 1948, and even before the 1987 constitutional revision, there had already been eight revisions—a sign of our political backwardness then. Since the 1987 revision, however, we have enjoyed a relatively stable period of over 20 years without any change in the constitution, and this corresponds, not surprisingly, to the period after the transition to democracy.

There are, of course, some aspects of the current constitution that we may feel are inconvenient or wanting in some ways. Yet when we ask ourselves whether there are really urgent reasons for changing it, which would justify going through the cumbersome and complicated process of the revision at this juncture, the answers provided by the advocates of revision are, as we have examined, unpersuasive. Therefore, I am opposed to revising the constitution now. In addition to my counterarguments, I am opposed to the current discussions on constitutional revision for the following three reasons.

First, we should guard against using the talk of constitutional revision as a political tool. Most arguments for revision proposed by politicians fall under this category. A prime example would be the proposal to change to a parliamentary system that was promised during the DJP coalition government between Kim Dae Jung and Kim Jong Pil. Even though some plausible arguments were offered in favor of parliamentarism, most people in Korea were able to figure out that the real purpose of the proposed revision was to make possible power-sharing between the two people. There are other examples from the past in which constitutional revisions were proposed to restructure

the whole political landscape through a realignment of political factions. The recent proposals for constitutional revision sound danger-
ously similar to these past attempts. That is why I believe that everyone should stop misleading and confusing the people right now with
any more arguments over constitutional revision.

With almost all past presidents, toward the end of their term
arguments for a change to a parliamentary system were inevitably
raised. This stemmed from the political calculation by the incumbents
that a parliamentary system would allow them to continue to have an
influence in the National Assembly after they leave office and that
this would ensure a better chance of avoiding political retribution
than would allowing a new president to take power. Especially when
a change of parties is seen as a real possibility, the incumbent is likely
to be seriously attracted to the idea of switching to a parliamentary
system. Using constitutional revision as a political tool in this way
must be resisted.

Second, we must guard against arguments for revision that seek
to tamper with the core principles of the constitution relating to the
ideological foundation and identity of the Republic of Korea. The core
values enshrined in our constitution are a liberal democracy and a
market economy based on respect for individuals' rights and autonomy. The history of humankind is proving these to be universal values
that most people of the world are aspiring to realize.

The recent arguments for constitutional revision are mostly aimed
at partial changes pertaining to the single-term presidency, the syn-
chronization of electoral terms, and replacing the prime ministership
with the vice presidency. Slightly more ambitious arguments call for
a change in the structure of the government. There are other arguments relating to the more fundamental aspects of the state, such as
calls for revising the articles on national territory, national unification,
international peace, and the economic order. One even hears calls
for reconsidering the article on liberal democracy.

If discussions for revision were to open under the pretext of de-

liberating on arguments for partial revision, there is a possibility that
they would be overtaken by the more vocal leftist forces who claim
to give preference to national unification over individual rights, equality over freedom, and self-reliance over alliance and who will not be
shy about undermining the core constitutional values of liberal democracy and market economy. As a result, arguments would be introduced for revising the constitution to adopt as its highest ideal
unification with North Korea or a socialistic obsession over equality,
and this would create a serious division among people and aggravate
social conflicts. It would be a true national disaster if the leftists
decided to cause such division and conflict as a means for a political
breakthrough during the next presidential election. In sum, we must
be ever-vigilant about grave attempts to destroy the constitution mas-
querading as arguments for a constitutional revision and prevent them
from overtaking the debate.

Third, we must guard against the fatal conceit of attempting to
create a perfect constitution through revision. Calls for a constitution
"more suitable for the 21st century" fall under this category. Since
our first constitution in 1948, we have gone through more than half
a century of constitutional revisions and violations of constitutional
order to finally create our current constitution. Today, the constitution is no longer a bundle of dead letters, but a living norm—a supreme law—that grounds our rights, freedom, and happiness and that
regulates the powers of the state. The constitution has become what
it is by a process of refinement and elaboration through interpretation
and application to a continuously changing history with its myriad
political, social, and economic contexts.

In light of this, how should we think about the proposal to create
from someone's desktop an ideal constitution, a perfect constitution
that is more suitable for the 21st century? Is that humanly possible?
Human reason is limited, and each of us possesses only a restricted
range of experience, wisdom, and information. It is impossible to at-

tain the level reason, fullness of experience, wisdom, and information required to create a perfect constitution.

To begin with, people have different ideas about what a perfect constitution is and what is required to make it suitable for the 21st century. Moreover, the constitution must last over time and be relevant for future generations, yet regarding the future and our posterity, we in the present are behind a true "veil of ignorance." How are we to make a perfect constitution that takes into consideration every future development? The very idea that we could make an ideal constitution is an expression of arrogance or, to use Friedrich Hayek's expression, "fatal conceit."

When I see such idealistic arguments for constitutional revision, I cannot help but think of them in relation to certain misguided views on "reform" commonly found in Korean society. As between the ideal and reality, reform belongs in the realm of reality. The ideal gives us hope and expectations regarding the future and is absolutely vital for any human society. That which is ideal need not always be practically realizable; indeed, some ideals are all the more attractive because they are unrealistic and fantastic.

Reform, on the other hand, is the human endeavor to make society a better place in reality. Given a "reform" plan that sets up a utopian society as the goal and seeks to bring it about in one fell stroke and another reform plan that seeks to move gradually toward a better society based upon the consensus of its members, which one is the more realistic and practicable? The former is close to what Karl Popper referred to as "utopian social engineering" and the latter as "piecemeal social engineering." For us humans with limited intellect and capability, it is difficult enough even to imagine what a utopian society would look like. It is utterly impossible for us to make it a reality. Therefore, to advocate a utopian "reform" is to insist obstinately and conceitedly that the impossible is possible. It is political deception. It is fatal conceit because, in the name of realizing the impossible, it will bring about only turmoil and catastrophe in the society. The Bolshevik revolution and other communist social engineering projects of the past are examples of the destruction of lives and livelihoods committed in the name of some utopian dream, whether called the dictatorship of the proletariat or the working class's paradise.

Currently in Korea, leftists are arguing for "reform" every chance they get—reform for a complete "liquidation" of the era of the rightists and reform for realizing the goals of self-reliance and social equality. Projects for "settling the past," heavy taxations for the purpose of reducing polarization of wealth, and the policy of downward equalization of education—all of which are key policy goals of the current administration—may be understood in this context. We must guard against the fatal conceit of such pseudo-reform rhetoric.

The same is true with "reforming" the constitution. A constitution is not an idealistic blueprint for a perfect utopia. It is a norm that makes our daily lives possible, and any reform of the constitution must be grounded in reality and proceed on a piecemeal basis to make it fit better with our lives. We should not engage in any talk of a chimerical ideal constitution or of a more perfect constitution better suited for the 21st century, which will only promote national discord and discontent. If some parts of the constitution turn out to require improvement, the Constitutional Court should first endeavor to accommodate the demand through constitutional interpretation. If the improvement cannot be made through interpretation, then parts may be revised on the basis of a national consensus gradually and in stages. That is the proper way to proceed.

## Conclusion

I have examined the arguments in favor of a constitutional revision and have offered my reasons for opposing them. My impression from the current discussions on changing the constitution is that people tend to conclude that problems arising from mismanagement of institutions are problems of the institutions themselves, and as a result, think that changing the institutions will solve the problem. Whatever problems we are facing now in national politics are not due to any problems with the constitution, but to mismanagement of politics and lack of statesmanship skills. No constitution, or any institution, can embody perfect truth or perfect beauty. It is up to the people who implement them and apply them to the specific contexts.

In addition, I would like to stress that now is not the time for politicians to be talking about changing the constitution. For any future possibility of actual revision, it is desirable and necessary for scholars and other experts to engage in a free and open-ended discussion about revising the constitution. Political leaders should be concentrating on matters of more immediate and perhaps greater concern for the Korean nation.

Korea is finding itself unable to navigate the East Asian regional environment, which is becoming more and more volatile due to North Korea's development of the nuclear bomb and other weapons of mass destruction. This was shown graphically during the missile-launching incident in 2006. As soon as North Korea launched the missiles, the United States and Japan immediately traced the missile's trajectory under their joint defense system, and as follow-up measures hastened to refer the matter to the U.N. Security Council and to develop a missile defense system. As for China and Russia, they rushed to develop cutting-edge weapons in response to the U.S.–Japanese missile defense system, which is triggering an arms race, or a power struggle, among the great powers surrounding the Korean Peninsula.

In this environment, the Roh Moo Hyun government neglected the Korea–U.S. alliance and the cooperation between Korea, United States, and Japan while boasting of "autonomous diplomacy" and "self-reliant national defense." The result is that Korea was a loner not accepted into any circles and, miserably enough, even scorned by North Korea. When peace on the Korean Peninsula is gravely threatened by North Korea's reckless and unpredictable behavior, how are we going to handle such a crisis and how will we survive? Is it just my oversensitivity to be reminded of the tragic history of a century ago when we tried to chart an independent course in the midst of a power struggle among the neighboring imperialist powers and ultimately lost our national sovereignty?

On top of this, our national competitiveness has been falling continuously. Recently, there was deplorable news: According to a survey by the IMD Business School in Switzerland, Korea's competitiveness ranking fell from 29th in 2005 to 38th in 2006, and the government's efficiency ranking went down 16 steps. In other words, Korea is faced with crisis-level threats from both within and without. How are we to prepare for these threats and save the nation? This is the urgent task that politicians should be struggling to solve. Now is not the time to be idly discussing constitutional revisions.

CHAPTER TWO

# Uneasy About the Rule of Law: Reconciling Constitutionalism and "Participatory Democracy"

## Haim Chaihark

### Introduction

On a number of occasions since 2003, the Constitutional Court of Korea has found itself at the center of media attention. Although it has a relatively short history of decades, the court is by all accounts starting to exercise a great deal of influence over Korea's political processes. Indeed, to some of its critics, the Constitutional Court is becoming too political and too partisan, and its influence is sometimes criticized as excessive, particularly given that the members of court are not democratically elected. Its defenders, on the other hand, claim that the court has contributed significantly to transforming Korea into a country where rule of law is respected. Whether or not one likes the court's decisions, there is no denying that more and more controversial issues are being litigated and settled by the Constitutional Court. In other words, Koreans are increasingly experiencing constitutional politics in their daily lives.

One consequence of this "constitutionalization" of politics is an emerging debate over the proper relationship between rule of law and democracy. The Constitutional Court may have played a role in facilitating Korea's transition to democracy, but as people become more familiar with democracy, the fact that so many political issues are being resolved by the court is causing many to raise questions about the court's proper place in a democracy. This is also being spurred on by the perception that in a "full" democracy everything must be determined by the people. The demand for more participation by the people in every sector of society, which has been on the rise since the democratic transition in 1987, received a major boost under the presidency of Roh Moo Hyun (2003–2008), who elected to name his administration the "participatory government."

In a context where democracy has been the ultimate goal and overriding value for so long, people's participation can only be seen as a good thing. Most people are also accustomed to thinking that democracy must be accompanied by rule of law. To be sure, democracy and rule of law are desirable ideals that can be joined together in the fight against tyranny and dictatorship. Yet there is a point at which the two seem to part company. Generally speaking, democracy means popular sovereignty, and this includes the idea of giving full rein to the will of the people, which has supreme authority. By contrast, rule of law means, among other things, "government of law, not of men," which implies that there are certain things that cannot be done or disposed of even if the people desire it. Sometimes this ideal is expressed in terms of the supremacy of constitutional law. Most democratic countries of the world have a political system that tries to combine these two potentially conflicting ideals. The term "constitutional democracy" is used to refer to this system: The first half of the term points to the ideal of rule of law, and the latter half embodies the notion of popular sovereignty.

In the Korean context, although most people accept this ideal of constitutional democracy, there is at present a greater desire to strengthen the "democracy" part—so much so that rule of law is liable to be seen as an obstacle to the full implementation of democracy. To that extent, rule of law may appear to have questionable legitimacy as a political ideal for the Korean polity. In this era of "democracy after democratization,"[1] the most pressing task confronting Korea may be that of reconciling rule of law with democracy, or at least maintaining a proper balance between the two. In this article, I describe how the apparent "success" of the Constitutional Court is bringing into relief this tension between rule of law and democracy. The first section provides a brief account of the court's performance since its establishment following the democratic transition. This is followed in the second section by a discussion of several high-profile cases decided by the court, whose cumulative effect has been to highlight the tension inherent in the system of constitutional democracy. The third section is a description of recent efforts by the judiciary to accommodate the demands of democracy by expanding the avenues for people's participation. The article ends with an attempt to understand the situation within a larger theoretical framework.

## Korea's Constitutional Order Since 1987

The current Constitutional Court of Korea is a product of political negotiations during the process of revising the constitution in the aftermath of the so-called June Uprising which sparked the end of authoritarian rule and began the historic transition to democracy.[2] Yet whether to create a separate constitutional court was not a priority issue for the negotiators at the time. More political energy and resources were spent over such issues as: How long should the president's term be? Should the president be allowed to serve a second term? Should the National Assembly, Korea's parliament, have the power to inspect and investigate affairs of the state? What should be included in the section on the rights of individual citizens? In other

---

1. This is the title of a book published recently in Korea by one of its leading political scientists. Choi Jang-jip, *Minjuhwa ihuŭ i Minjujuŭ i* [Democracy After Democratization] (Seoul: Humanitas, 2004).

2. For a general description of the process of transition to democracy, see John Kie-chang Oh, *Korean Politics: The Quest for Democratization and Economic Development* (Ithaca, N.Y.: Cornell University Press, 1999).

words, the question of who should have the power to review the constitutionality of legislations did not receive much attention.

When it did receive some attention, the idea of creating a separate, European-style constitutional court was adopted almost as an afterthought. Given that the previous constitutions gave the power of constitutional review to an ad hoc Constitutional Committee that never had occasion to exercise that power, representatives of the opposition thought that the supreme court should be in charge of constitutional or judicial review as a way of strengthening the judiciary vis-à-vis the other branches of the government. As against this, the ruling party wanted to create a separate but weak institution that would be in charge of constitutional issues—something along the lines of the previous constitutions. A compromise was reached when the opposition agreed to creating a separate institution on the condition that it would have the power to adjudicate "constitutional complaints," which are petitions brought by individual citizens claiming that their constitutional rights were violated by the actions of the state.[3]

Thus, the Constitutional Court was established in 1988. But even after it was established, there were forces that prevented it from exercising much power. For example, the first Constitutional Court Act, which specified the structure and organization of the court, provided that only a small number of the justices of the court would be permanent, full-time members. Moreover, the court did not have much of a caseload at the beginning, due in part to the fact that the Korean public was unacquainted with its powers, and unsure of how they might benefit from using its services. One former justice of the court wrote that the justices at the time deliberately wrote long and detailed decisions on relatively minor issues so as to show the public that it was ready and willing to hear their grievances.[4]

    3. *The First Ten Years of the Korean Constitutional Court* (Seoul: The Constitutional Court of Korea, 2001) (available online at www.ccourt.go.kr/library/docu_material02.asp).
    4. Yi Shi-yun, "A Ten Years' Retrospective on Constitutional Adjudication,"

Over time, however, the court has become an extremely busy institution. The law was changed to authorize the appointment of nine full-time justices.[5] As of August 2004, the total number of cases filed with the Constitutional Court was 10,377, and after having dismissed about a third of these on technical grounds, the court rendered substantive decisions on the rest. Unlike the U.S. Supreme Court, which has the power to grant writs of certiorari to select and decide on only the most important constitutional issues, the Korean Constitutional Court is obligated to hear all cases filed at its docket. More significant, based on the number of cases in which the court rendered a decision finding that a legislation or a state action was unconstitutional, some commentators have used the label "activist" to describe the court's orientation.[6] Indeed, by striking down laws that were disrespectful of individual rights, the court has often been regarded as a champion of democracy. It was seen as undertaking the task of completing the democratic transition or, alternatively, of consolidating democracy after the initial transition.

Thus, it might even be argued that the Constitutional Court has attained the stature of the guardian of the constitution or *Hüter der Verfassung*.[7] It is certainly the case that more and more individuals

---

*Kong-pŏp Yŏngu* [Korean Public Law Research], vol. 27, no. 3 (June 1999) (in Korean).

5. While the nine Justices are formally appointed by the President, only three of the nine are actually chosen by the President. Of the remaining six, three are nominated by the Chief Justice of the Supreme Court, and the other three nominated by the National Assembly. Korean Constitution, art. 111, §§ 2 & 3. Of the three nominated by National Assembly, the practice has been that the ruling party chooses one, the number one opposition party chooses another, and the third chosen through a compromise between the ruling party and the opposition. Thus, if a Justice nominated by the Chief Justice of the Supreme Court retires, it is understood that that seat must be succeed by another justice chosen by the Chief Justice.

6. See, for example, Gavin Healey, "Judicial Activism in the New Constitutional Court of Korea," *Columbia Journal of Asian Law*, vol. 14, no. 2 (Spring 2000), pp. 213–234.

7. The term *Hüter der Verfassung* was made famous during the Weimar Republic in Germany when the two constitutional giants of the day, Hans Kelsen and Carl

are turning to the Constitutional Court to have their rights vindicated. On reflection, this is a remarkable feat on the part of the court, especially considering that many observers at the time of its establishment expressed skepticism about whether such an "anomalous" institution would survive at all. It was seen as an anomaly because although the system of maintaining a separate constitutional court has roots in European countries with parliamentary systems of government, the remainder of the Korean government structure was basically understood to be modeled on the American-style presidential system. Nevertheless, by presiding over the process of democratic consolidation, the court has also managed to consolidate Korea's constitutional order. The fact that Korea has not experienced a constitutional revision since 1987—the longest such period in modern Korean history—might be counted as an indication that the constitutional order has become firmly entrenched. It must be also noted that in the process, the court has transformed the constitution from a mere decorative parchment into a real, living norm regulating the everyday lives of the people as well as the operation of the government.

One measure of the consolidation of constitutional order, or of the fact that constitutional politics is taking root, might be the increasing popularity of the phrase "destruction of constitutional order." Popularized in the post-democratization period after the historic trial of the two ex-presidents Chun Doo Hwan and Roh Tae Woo in which their crimes were described as having destroyed the constitutional order,[8] the phrase has come to stand for one of the worst forms of

---

Schmitt engaged in a heated debate over who shall be the final guardian of the constitution when faced with a constitutional crisis.

    8. For a description of the unfolding of this case, see John Oh, *Korean Politics*, pp. 164–181; James M. West, "Martial Lawlessness: The Legal Aftermath of Kwangju," *Pacific Rim Law and Policy Journal*, vol. 6 (1997), pp. 85–168. See also David M. Waters, "Korean Constitutionalism and the 'Special Act' to Prosecute Former Presidents Chun Doo-Hwan and Roh Tae-Woo," *Columbia Journal of Asian Law*, vol. 10 (Fall, 1996), pp. 461–485; Hahm Chaihark, "Rule of Law in South Korea,"

political transgression that anyone can be charged with. It is at least arguable that this has also had the effect of deepening people's respect for the constitution as well as for the Constitutional Court. Also, as shown by recent political controversies discussed below, the fact that ordinary people and the politicians are routinely using this form of expression to attack their opponents indicates that at least at the rhetorical level, constitutionalism has become a virtue that must be defended by everybody.

## Court As the Protector of Constitutional Order

The Constitutional Court has gained quite a reputation as the final guardian of the constitution and its principles, and recently its decisions have begun to receive more attention from the media and the general public. This is so because during the past couple of years, it has had several occasions to decide on very controversial and divisive political issues. Apart from any fame or notoriety this has brought the court, these decisions are significant because they seem to signal a certain transition in the status of the court. As noted above, the court was generally seen as the champion of democracy during the first phase of operation. This was because in many cases it decided in favor of individuals who alleged that a specific law or state action had violated their constitutional rights. Yet as captured in the well-known phrase "counter-majoritarian difficulty,"[9] any court that takes a stance on constitutional grounds against the decisions of the democratically elected branches of the government is bound to face the issue of how to reconcile or negotiate the potentially divergent demands of constitutionalism on the one hand and democracy on the other. For although we commonly use the term "constitutional democracy" as an ideal that a modern polity should strive after, it is also a fact that the

---

in *Asian Discourses of Rule of Law*, ed. Randall Peerenboom (London: Routledge-Curzon, 2004), pp. 399–403.

9. As is well known, this phrase was made popular by Alexander M. Bickel. See his, *The Least Dangerous Branch* (New Haven, Conn.: Yale University Press, 1962).

two parts of that ideal may pull in different directions.[10] Most people agree that the will of the people must be the fount of political legitimacy, but centuries of experiment worldwide with democracy have also taught us that invocation of popular will to circumvent institutional requirements can often lead to unhappy consequences. The notion that there is a higher law, which not even the will of the majority can trump is thus essential to a thriving democratic polity. The idea is that sometimes even a democracy must be protected from itself.[11] Of course, a democratic constitution must be the product of the will of the people, but it must also be recognized that the constitution can set limits on the people's will. Moreover, there is a sense that the will of the people itself must be formed and "constituted" by and within the parameters of the constitution.[12]

It is therefore not surprising that ever since its inception, the modern Korean polity was designed as a constitutional democracy, rather than as a direct or popular democracy. Indeed, we might say that the primary goal of the democratic transition in 1987 was to achieve the correct balance between elements of democracy and constitutionalism. This is evident in the 1987 constitution itself. In order to empower democracy, particularly in light of past experience of authoritarian rule, the constitution strengthened the basic rights of the

10. Walter F. Murphy, "Constitutions, Constitutionalism, and Democracy," in *Constitutionalism and Democracy: Transitions in the Contemporary World*, ed. Douglas Greenberg et al. (New York: Oxford University Press, 1993), pp. 3–25; Ronald Dworkin, *Freedom's Law: The Moral Reading of the American Constitution* (Cambridge: Harvard University Press, 1996), pp. 15–19.

11. This is sometimes expressed through the idea of "self-binding." See Stephen Holmes, "Gag Rules or the Politics of Omission," in *Constitutionalism and Democracy*, ed. Jon Elster and Rune Slagstad (Cambridge: Cambridge University Press, 1988).

12. This is what Ulrich Preuss calls the "integrative" function of constitutions. See his *Constitutional Revolution: The Link between Constitutionalism and Progress*, trans. Deborah L. Schneider (Atlantic Highlands, N.J.: Humanities Press, 1995), p. 5. He also states that "The constitution gives birth to the people in the sense in which this notion has been developed for the concept of democracy, that is, in the sense of the demos." Ibid. p. 19.

people and restrained the powers of the government, particularly of the president, while giving more power to the National Assembly. And in order to buttress constitutionalism, it established an independent Constitutional Court, which can both rule on the constitutionality of legislation passed by the National Assembly and hear constitutional petitions filed by individual citizens.

In the initial phase of democratic consolidation, however, with the Constitutional Court demanding heightened respect for individual rights, democracy and constitutionalism seemed to go hand in hand. What the recent decisions suggest is that this cozy and comfortable relationship may be coming to an end, or at least to a point at which the relationship must be redefined. For in a series of decisions rendered since the late 2003, the court has started to carve out, in the name of the constitution, a stance that required going against the democratically elected branches of the government and perhaps a large segment of the Korean people as well.

### The Confidence Referendum Case

The first suggestion came with a case in which the Constitutional Court had to decide upon a constitutional complaint filed by several individuals who claimed that certain pronouncements by President Roh Moo Hyun had violated their rights. Reflecting his political style of "speaking directly to the people," whenever his popularity seemed to be declining or whenever the opposition criticized his policies, Roh had repeatedly bypassed existing institutional arrangements, including his own party, to appeal directly to the people. One such instance was his promising to seek the people's confidence after the completion of his first year in office. He also seriously suggested holding a national referendum as a means for verifying the people's confidence. Unhappy with Roh's populist approach, a number of his political opponents filed a constitutional complaint with the court claiming that the president's proposal to use the national referendum as a vote of confidence was unconstitutional.[13]

One of the basic principles of the current constitution is that Korea shall have a presidential system of government rather than a parliamentary one. Although certain elements of the parliamentary system are incorporated into the current constitution,[14] the Constitutional Court has consistently interpreted it to ordain a presidential system with a set term of office for the president. Thus, although Roh Moo Hyun's suggestion to leave office upon a vote of nonconfidence by the people may have been an expression of his respect for the people's voice, to his foes it was no more than an expression of his disrespect for the constitution. For according to the constitution, a national referendum may be called only to ask the people's will on specific policy issues of great importance, such as those relating to foreign affairs, national defense, and national unification.[15] Thus to many of his critics, Roh's proposing to submit the "issue" of his confidence to a national referendum not only was showing indifference or contempt for the constitution, but was also revealing a dangerous tendency toward plebiscitary politics.

In the end, the case was actually decided in the president's favor because the majority of the justices thought that the president's proposal did not amount to an exercise of state power, which must exist before a valid constitutional petition can be filed. Since there was no state action that could have violated the rights of the petitioners, the case was dismissed for failing to meet the threshold requirement.

13. Case Nos. 2003 HŏnMa 694, 700, and 742 (consolidated) (judgment of Nov. 27, 2003).

14. For example, the National Assembly has the power to recommend to the president the removal of the prime minister and other cabinet ministers. Also, members of the National Assembly may be appointed by the president to serve as a cabinet minister.

15. The only other time a national referendum is contemplated by the current constitution is when a bill to revise the constitution has passed the National Assembly by a two-thirds majority of its total members.

Nevertheless, a minority of the justices argued that the president's proposal constituted a clear statement of a concrete intention to carry out a series of government actions, which taken together would constitute an unconstitutional exercise of the presidential power to call a national referendum. Further, it stated that when carried out, the president's plan would inevitably result in the violation of the petitioners' right to political participation according to lawful procedure and the right to be free of coerced expression of one's political opinion. More significant, the minority opinion basically issued a warning against using the national referendum as a political means to rally support for the president's position by saying that such a "vote of confidence" not only would seriously distort the will of the people but would also become a cover for authoritarian politics. Furthermore, the fact that the decision was badly split (5 to 4) indicated an increasing concern regarding President Roh's attitude toward the current constitution and the principles it represents.

### The Presidential Impeachment Case

If the decision in the "vote of confidence" case was rather muted in its criticism of the president, a later case provided occasion for the court to express a stronger disapproval of the president's actions. Indeed, the Constitutional Court explicitly declared that Roh's mere proposal to use the national referendum in a manner not contemplated by the constitution (i.e., as a vote of confidence) was a violation of his duty to uphold the constitution. Even though the proposal did not result in a direct violation of anyone's constitutional rights, the court seemed to be saying, the proposal itself was nonetheless a violation of the constitution. The majority justices warned that Article 72 of the constitution, which grants the president the power to submit certain issues to a national referendum, must be interpreted narrowly and strictly so as to prevent it from being abused as a political tool to bolster the president's approval ratings.[16]

16. Case No. 2004 HŏnNa 1 (judgment of May 14, 2004).

The case in which the court issued this warning arose from the impeachment proceeding instituted by the National Assembly against President Roh. As was widely reported around world, in March 2004, Roh Moo Hyun became the first sitting president in Korean history to be impeached by a resolution passed by the National Assembly. The constitution, however, is clear: The final decision on whether or not to uphold the impeachment resolution had to be made by the Constitutional Court. Until that time, the powers of the president were suspended and the prime minister was appointed acting president.

The first of many events that culminated in the impeachment crisis took place in December 2003. On the first anniversary of his election, President Roh attended an evening street-rally organized by his ardent political supporters, mostly members of the so-called Nosamo (Korean acronym for "Gathering of People Who Love Roh Moo Hyun") which had played a critical role in his election to the presidency. In his address to his supporters, Roh urged them to come out in the general election in April 2004 to complete the "citizens' revolution" they had started together a year before. At this, the two main opposition parties (the Grand National Party and the Millennium Democratic Party) immediately responded with an outcry that the agitation was not only politically inappropriate, but also illegal in light of Korea's strict election laws.

At a couple of press conferences in February 2004, Roh expressed hope that the "voters would give overwhelming support" to a minority party composed of his supporters (Uri Open Party) in the upcoming April general election. He also pledged that he would do all that was humanly possible to give aid to the Uri Open Party. As innocent as it may sound politically, from a legal standpoint this could be seen as problematic because Korean election laws explicitly forbid all public officials, including the president, from influencing, let alone interfering with, election processes. Indeed, within one week the National Elections Committee, a constitutional agency established to

ensure clean and fair elections, announced that Roh's remarks constituted a violation of the president's duty to remain neutral in relation
to elections. Yet on the following day, Roh in effect defied the committee's decision in a public speech by calling the ruling nonsensical
as well as pledging to stake everything on the outcome of the general
elections. Led by the Millennium Democratic Party, the opposition
once again demanded the president's neutrality and strongly suggested the possibility of instituting an impeachment proceeding.
When Roh defiantly refused to comply with the opposition's demands, an impeachment resolution was actually introduced in the
National Assembly on March 9, setting the constitutional process in
motion.

Even at that point, Roh still had a chance to cope with the situation for there remained a period of 72 hours until the National
Assembly would vote on the resolution. Indeed, a simple apology and
a promise of neutrality would have sufficed to defuse the bomb. The
opposition parties were also showing some signs of reluctance to go
through with the vote. Nonetheless, on March 11, in a lengthy special
address aired live on television, Roh provocatively refused to apologize
or comply with the committee's decision. On March 12, against the
efforts of the Uri Open Party lawmakers to physically block the vote,
the two opposition parties passed the impeachment resolution.

In its decision, rendered on May 14, the Constitutional Court
found that on at least three counts the president had violated the
law. First, Roh's remarks at a couple of press conferences in which
he openly courted the people's support for the Uri Open Party, of
which he was not even a member, were in violation of Article 9 of
the Law on the Election of Public Officials and the Prevention of
Election Frauds, which provides that government officials shall maintain neutrality and not exercise influence over election matters. The
court emphasized that the president is a public servant whose duties
lie toward the entire citizenship of Korea and not just to those who
voted for him or his party. Second, his defiance of the ruling of the

National Elections Committee that he had violated the duty of neutrality constituted a violation of the president's duty to uphold the
constitution and practice rule of law. The court noted that as the
highest public official, the president's attitude toward the legal system
and other state agencies will inevitably influence that of his subor-
dinates and the general public. The constitutional status of the president therefore must be one of a role model in terms of respecting
the rule of law. Third, as mentioned above, his statement that he was
going to call a national referendum to measure people's confidence
in him also constituted a violation of his constitutional duty to uphold
constitution.

Ultimately, however, the court held that none of these offenses
committed by President Roh amounted to an impeachable crime that
warranted the extreme and only remedy of removing him from office.
According to Article 65 of the constitution, the president and other
high-ranking officials may be impeached by the National Assembly
for violating the constitution or national statutes in the performance
of official duty. And although the Constitutional Court found that
the president had violated both the constitution and a national statute, it reasoned that in order to "convict" him, the gravity of the
violations and the harm they posed to the constitutional order must
be weighed against the consequences of removing a democratically
elected president from office. It reasoned that the violations must be
of sufficient gravity to justify such an extreme remedy. In the end,
the court concluded that Roh's transgressions, although serious, could
not be seen as part of a deliberate and purposeful plan to subvert the
constitutional order; nor can they be deemed to have fundamentally
threatened the "free and democratic basic order," the highest value
and principle enshrined in the constitution.

The court ended its decision with a stern admonition to the president regarding his responsibilities toward the constitution:

The president's power and his political authority are derived from the constitution, and a president who disregards the constitution undermines and destroys his own power and authority. Especially in our situation where due to the short history of democratic politics the people's awareness of the constitution is only just beginning to blossom and where respect for the constitution has yet to take firm root in the minds of the people, the president's strong determination to defend the constitution cannot be overemphasized. As an "emblem of rule of law and respect for the law," the president must of course respect and obey the constitution and the laws personally, but beyond that, by taking firm action against the unconstitutional or unlawful acts of other state agencies and the general public, the president should strive to realize the rule of law and ultimately defend the free and democratic basic order of the state.[17]

In addition, on many occasions, the Constitutional Court underscored its own role and authority under the current constitutional framework. For example, it emphasized that the power to find a statute unconstitutional lies solely with the Constitutional Court, such that even if the president is unhappy with an existing law, he has the duty to obey and enforce it unless and until it is found unconstitutional by the court or amended by the legislature. Also, it proclaimed that in an impeachment proceeding, the "constitution" against which the official's behavior is to be measured includes not only the provisions of the written text, but also the principles established through the court's own precedents. In another place, it asserted that it has the freedom to frame the legal issues without being bound by the arguments presented in the National Assembly's impeachment resolution. These may be minor or technical points, but through these the court seems to be trying to reiterate its own authority under the constitution and to ensure that it is not challenged by anyone.[18] Fur-

17. *Hŏnpŏp Jaep'anso Pallyejip* [Constitutional Court Report], vol. 16, no. 2, pp. 656–657.

18. For an analysis of this case comparing it with the American constitutional system, see Youngjae Lee, Law, Politics, and Impeachment: The Impeachment of Roh Moo-hyun from a Comparative Constitutional Perspective, *American Journal of Comparative Law*, vol. 53, no. 2 (Spring 2005).

ther, they might be read as an indication that the court is beginning
to regard itself as the sole guardian of the constitutional order.

## The Capital Relocation Case

A more recent case in which the Constitutional Court further ex-
pounded on its role within the constitutional order was decided on
October 21, 2004.[19] In this decision, the court articulated a controversial theory of "customary constitution," something similar to what
the British call "constitutional conventions." The decision was controversial because Korea, unlike the United Kingdom, has a single
documentary constitution that is understood to be the highest law of
the land. Moreover, the written constitution has more than a hundred
articles and covers a fairly extensive range of issues in some detail.
The court itself had always endeavored to ground its holdings in one
or another of the textual provisions of the constitution. But beyond
its novelty, the theory of customary constitution was even more noteworthy for its implications for the court's status.

The dispute started when the Roh Moo Hyun administration
pushed through the National Assembly a law whose purpose was the
creation of a new "administrative capital" in a region south of Seoul.
As far as President Roh was concerned, he was merely carrying out
one of his campaign pledges, and as far as the politicians in the
National Assembly—including members of the opposition—were
concerned, passing the law was considered a strategically clever move
to attract voters from the region in which the new capital was expected to be built. Yet a number of citizens brought a constitutional
complaint claiming, among other things, that this special law violated
their constitutional right to exercise their vote at a referendum on
issues of major national significance. The argument was that the location of a nation's capital is a matter of constitutional importance

19. Case No. 2004 HŏnMa 554 (judgment of Oct. 21, 2004).

and that a national referendum should be held on whether to move the capital to a new location.

The National Assembly had passed the law authorizing the creation of a new administrative capital in late 2003, before the impeachment crisis, when politicians on both sides of the aisle thought agreeing to the bill would cultivate votes in the Chungcheong province, where the new capital was to be built. But by the summer of 2004, the political terrain had altered considerably, and the opposition were either arguing for a revision of the law or explicitly opposing the relocation of the capital. What had happened in the intervening time were the impeachment proceeding, which lasted from March to May, and, more important, the general elections in April, in which the fledgling Uri Open Party of the president's loyal supporters gained the majority in the National Assembly and the two opposition parties lost many seats. After regaining his powers through the Constitutional Court's decision on the impeachment case, President Roh began to push his government to go through with the implementation of the capital relocation plan. In July 2004, several citizens filed constitutional complaints, and the opposition politicians were now backing this effort to block the plan.

The complainants argued that the capital relocation plan was unconstitutional for many reasons. First, they said, their right to vote had been violated because according to the constitution, matters of national importance must be approved by a national referendum. Next, they argued, the decision to move the capital should have been preceded by a nationwide opinion-gathering as well as a public hearing, and thus the law was a violation of their due process rights. The complainants also argued that since the relocation would be funded by taxpayers' money, they would be unlawfully forced to support a measure to which they had never consented.

When the Constitutional Court finally rendered its decision, it caused quite a stir. It held that the law was indeed unconstitutional. From a political standpoint, this in itself was significant because the court was siding with the opposition parties and going directly against the president and the ruling party. In the two cases discussed above, the court issued a strong warning against the president and even found him to have violated the constitution, but in the end, it had stopped short of a decision that actually contradicted his position. In this case, however, the court appeared to have considered it its mission to make a clear statement that the president and the government were going too far. This is particularly so in light of the fact that the president and his supporters had put so much effort into arguing for the need for and the legitimacy of moving to a new capital. Casting its opponents as members of the conservative, or even reactionary, establishment thwarting its attempt to correct the regional imbalance of development, the Roh administration had all but turned this issue into a symbol of its reform policy. The justices of the Constitutional Court must have been aware of this when they were deliberating on the case. In other words, by issuing a decision striking down the capital relocation law, the Constitutional Court was no doubt aware that it was going against the will of a popularly elected president, a president who seemed to have received an indirect endorsement through the recent parliamentary election. This may be read as a sign that the court was now realizing that its role necessarily involves sometimes contradicting, in the name of the constitution, the popularly elected representatives of the people. This observation becomes more plausible when one considers the legal reasoning behind the court's holding.

Indeed, the court's decision attracted much commentary, from scholars as well as the media, for its articulation of a rather bold theory, which in turn allowed the court to claim the status of the final arbiter of constitutional meaning. The court said that the relocation law was unconstitutional because it attempted to achieve through normal legislation something that could only be done through a revision of the constitution itself. Its reasoning was that the location of the nation's capital is a constitutional issue, and although the current constitution does not specify Seoul as the seat of the nation's capital, the court stated that Seoul's status as the capital has been accepted by the people for generations such that it has become part of what the court called "customary constitution." It further reasoned that in order to change this state of affairs, one must go through the official process of revising, or amending, the constitution as stipulated in Articles 128 through 130 of the current constitution. Thus, in the end, it agreed with the complainants' argument that a national referendum was required because one of the procedures that is needed in order to revise the constitution is having the revised draft ratified by the people through a referendum.

This was noteworthy and problematic, in many respects. Most obviously, the idea of a customary constitution, although not entirely unfamiliar to students of constitutional law, had never been pronounced and used as the basis for a constitutional decision. As expected, the decision sparked much debate on the nature, source, and even existence of such norm, and the propriety of using it to strike down a duly legislated statute. Yet, from the viewpoint of constitutional politics, the most significant aspect of the decision was that the court was now explicitly positioning itself to be the sole interpreter and "discoverer" of the constitution. Although the decision nowhere states the procedure for identifying norms that have the status of customary constitution, it is clear that the court thinks that it is the one and only institution with the power to say what is or is not customary constitutional law. This is significant because this would from now on allow the court to strike down statutes passed by the National Assembly even if it cannot provide any basis in the text of the written constitution. All it needs to do is to say that the law in question violates some hitherto unidentified customary constitutional law. From a cynical point of view, a practice or a fact may suddenly take on constitutional importance whenever the court recognizes it as a long-standing tradition and labels it a customary constitution.

This would in effect enable the court not only to interpret the existing constitution, but also to define and discover new constitutional laws.

On the more positive side, the decision signals a court that is willing to take on the elected branches of the government. It may be a sign that the court is searching for a new role in the political system, with the realization that its own legitimacy is grounded in something other than popular democratic support. Indeed, as predicted, many supporters of the president and the ruling party vehemently criticized the court, some even charging that a government agency that contradicts the will of the people should be abolished. Just when people are feeling proud of and empowered by the nation's political achievements since the democratic transition, the critics seemed to say, the court is revealing itself as an elitist, conservative, and antidemocratic institution. Thus, in a context within which democracy is counted as the overarching value and the ultimate source of legitimacy, the court is faced with the difficult task of articulating a role for itself. It perhaps is becoming clearer to both the court and the people that constitutionalism can sometimes come in conflict with democracy. This of course is nothing new to constitutional scholars, but to a public that has been accustomed to thinking of the Constitutional Court as a champion of democratic causes, this may be a new (and perhaps rude) awakening. The court's decision in this case will have done a public service if it spurs on the Korean public to think more deeply about the place of the Constitutional Court in a democratic system and, more broadly, about the relationship between constitutionalism and democracy.[20]

20. It should be noted that after this decision by the Constitutional Court, the government passed an amended version of the statute in question, which was also challenged by many as unconstitutional. The major difference between the new law and the old law that was struck down was that many government agencies, including the President's Office, the National Assembly, the Supreme Court, and the Constitutional Court were now to remain in Seoul. In other words, the new law mandated the relocation of only the administrative branch, i.e., the Prime Minister's Office and various ministries, to the new site. The Constitutional Court declared that this did

## Rule of Law and "Participatory Democracy"

As mentioned above, the Constitutional Court has been largely successful in consolidating the constitutional order that was founded after the democratic transition. It has established a reputation as an agency that is sympathetic to the position and grievances of individuals who claim that their rights have been violated. It is even taking on the role of defending the constitution against any potential or real threat from other branches of government.

One result of this "success" is that the court is now increasingly being put in a situation in which it has to articulate a position that is in tension with, if not in opposition to, certain conceptions of democracy. That is, it is being portrayed as an institution that lacks democratic legitimacy. Supporters of President Roh during his impeachment proceedings openly questioned whether it was democratically justifiable to let nine unelected elite justices decide the fate of a popularly elected president. Indeed, one of the self-proclaimed goals of the Roh Moo Hyun government is to expand the scope of people's participation in the government. The idea obviously has a natural appeal. Particularly in light of the recent interest among political theorists in "deliberative democracy," the notion that more people with diverse backgrounds and viewpoints should come together to deliberate on affairs of the government would not be resisted by anybody.

---

not violate the constitution. Case No. 2005 HŏnMa 579 (judgment of Nov. 24, 2005). Seven of the nine justices said that the new city to be built in the Chungcheong Province does not amount to a new capital, and therefore the petitioners' claim that a constitutional revision is required was without merit. Interestingly, three of those seven also went out of their way to indicate that there was no such thing as a "customary constitution" that says Seoul shall be the seat of the nation's capital. Commentators noted that these three had all been appointed to the Court after Roh Moo-hyun became president, implying that they were following the "party line."

*Lay Participation in Adjudication*

As it is practiced in the Korean context, however, this idea of increased participation is causing a number of problems for the ideal of rule of law, and especially the judiciary. For example, one likely casualty, perhaps unintended, of emphasizing participation is the idea of professionalism. The notion that certain tasks require special skills or long training that ordinary people are not likely to possess is liable to be seen as mere elitist rhetoric designed to exclude the people's voice, viewpoints, and interests. Similarly, seniority in the workplace can be seen at best as nothing but a tool for maintaining the status quo and at worst as a relic of the past actively impeding innovation and the introduction of new ideas. Thus, the idea of "participatory democracy" advocated by the Roh regime, as well as the reforms undertaken in pursuit thereof, seem almost to require the rejection of professionalism and disregard for seniority.

Obviously, this has a damaging effect on people in the various professions, especially those in government service, such as career bureaucrats and diplomats. They are often identified as the "targets" of reform. Indeed, in many government agencies under the executive branch of the government, the head positions have been filled with those who have a populist outlook, without regard to their rank. Yet the government branch likely to suffer the most from such antiprofessionalist position is the judiciary, in which specialized knowledge in the law and the seniority system have played a vital role in maintaining the current system.[21] The judges and the court system in

---

21. The Public Prosecutors comprise the other government sector made up of legal professionals with similar specialization and structure. Yet, the prosecutors are a part—albeit a very large part—of the Ministry of Justice, which in turn is part of the executive branch under the direct control of the President. In other words, they have already been targeted by Roh's "reform" measures when he appointed as Minister of Justice a woman attorney (Kang Keum-sil) in private practice much junior in terms of the bar-passage year to the head of the public prosecutors. Subsequent ministers of justice have also been appointed without regard to their "rank" as measured according to the time passed since they took the national bar exam.

general are now becoming the targets of antiprofessionalism and efforts to subvert the seniority system.

One example of this trend is the increasing interest shown by the government (as well as a few citizen groups) in jury trials (*baesimje* in Korean) commonly found in Anglo-American law and the system of lay judges (*chamsimje*) found in Germany and other European jurisdictions. The relative benefits and drawbacks of these are receiving serious attention by many because they both represent a potential means of introducing citizen participation in the operation of the judiciary. Advocates believe these should be adopted, in one form or another, for a number of reasons. For starters, such citizen participation in the administration of justice is said to enhance the democratic legitimacy of the judiciary, thereby bringing about a closer relationship between the people and the courts. Advocates claim that people will be more likely to accept court decisions if laypeople participate in the process. They also claim that lay participation will ensure that the decisions are based on the common sense of ordinary people and will prevent professional judges from departing too far from the people's sense of justice. Sometimes these proposals are advocated for almost the exact opposite reason. Especially in the case of lay judges, proponents of this system argue that it will allow the professional judges to draw on certain specialized knowledge that they may lack but which may be possessed by a layperson.

Whatever the theoretical justification, the ideological motivation behind the arguments is the idea that popular participation is a good thing even in the interpretation and application of the law. One of the core agenda of the Presidential Commission on Judicial Reform (PCJR) under the Roh administration was the implementation of some form of popular participation in adjudication. The PCJR has drafted and proposed to the National Assembly a bill titled "Law Concerning Citizens' Participation in Criminal Trials." The PCJR even conducted a couple of mock criminal trials in major cities of the country in which a jury of laypersons chosen by random sampling participated in the assessment of guilt as well as making recommendations on sentencing. These mock trials caused a few skeptics to express reservations about the introduction of juries, especially in light of the ongoing debates in the United States on the role of juries.

The Roh Moo Hyun government nevertheless insisted on introducing some form of jury trials. If the bill passed the legislature, criminal cases of a certain gravity would be tried before a jury of five to nine persons. The government intended to limit the number of jury trials to between 100 and 200 per year at first, then gradually expand the availability of jury trials after assessing the success of the new system.[22] Proponents of this change were confident that this had the support of the people and indeed was something that was required if Korea was to achieve full democracy. For them, the time had come for Koreans to stop entrusting their lives to a small group of professional jurists and to start relying on the wisdom of the people, which had time and again been proven correct. According to a survey commissioned in 2005 by the PCJR, a majority of citizens seemed to think that participation in adjudication would bring more democratic legitimacy to the courts and ultimately enhance the people's respect for the judiciary.[23]

The idea of incorporating some form of lay participation in judicial proceedings also received support from the judiciary itself, which made efforts to reform and project the image of citizen-friendly courts. The supreme court announced that starting in 2007 it would draw up a list of lay specialists in various fields who would be consulted regularly for their expertise in cases requiring knowledge in a specialized field. This was one of the ways in which the supreme court responded to the demands of the new and highly specialized

22. According to the proposed bill, if defendant does not wish to be tried by a jury, he or she has the option to be tried according to the existing system.

23. A summary of the survey results is available online at the website of the Presidential Committee on Judicial Reform: www.pcjr.go.kr/notice_view.asp ?tablename=home_notice&idx=107&gubun=02&page=1&strtype1=&strtype2=

economic and scientific environment Koreans lived in. As more cases are brought to the courts that require expertise beyond the scope of knowledge possessed by regular judges, there is a need for the courts to be better equipped to adjudicate such cases.

Politically speaking, this is an attempt to enhance the people's trust and respect for the courts by way of increasing the participation of people who are not professional jurists. It cannot be denied that there is a popular perception that the judiciary is made up of people of privileged background and who are therefore likely to be more conservative than the average Korean citizen. The supreme court's proposal thus stems from the view that more popular participation in the court proceedings will bring the judiciary that much closer to the people, which will in turn cause people to accept the rulings of the courts with more alacrity.

For critics, however, the dangers of this proposal may outweigh the expected benefits. They claim that this will undermine rule of law. Allowing experts to participate in the deliberation of the final decision has the potential to infringe upon the parties' constitutional right to be tried by judges who are qualified under the constitution and relevant statutes.[24] Further, the constitution provides that each judge shall rule independently according to the constitution and the laws.[25] Lay participation in the courts has the potential to violate this principle of judicial independence because the experts' testimonies and/or evaluations may have the effect of influencing or even determining the final outcome of the case. This would be particularly problematic in sensitive cases that reflect a deep-rooted schism within the society, such as those dealing with politically and ideologically divisive issues. If the experts are seen as representatives of a partisan group or advocates of a particular interest, people will no longer be disposed

24. Article 27 of the Korean Constitution guarantees every citizen the right to a trial by qualified judges in accordance with the law.

25. Article 103 is generally understood as a proclamation that every judge must be independent and free of outside influences.

to accept the decision of the court as impartial. Ultimately, rather than enhancing the trust that people have in the courts, this will only undermine that trust. When courts lose the trust of the people, the rule of law is bound to suffer.

### People's Participation in Judicial Appointments

Another example of the increasing tension between rule of law and participatory democracy is the demand that judicial appointments be more open to input and influence from citizen groups. For the proponents of participatory democracy, the traditional system in which judges basically get promoted through the hierarchy of the national court system is too closed and too conservative. The fact that the chief justice of the supreme court has ultimate control over the appointment and promotion of ordinary judges is seen as contributing to a system in which preference is inevitably given to judges who are deferential to their "seniors" and rarely challenge the settled interpretations of the law and the constitution. The argument is that judges with more innovative approaches to legal interpretation or willingness to question established practices of the judiciary are systematically disadvantaged, and that this results in the higher-level courts being staffed with only "deferential" judges. In other words, the argument is that in order to make the judiciary more diverse in its leanings, the appointment system must be reformed to allow ways for judges with different political agendas to get promoted to higher-level courts. This has been receiving support from inside the judiciary as well. In addition to citizen groups, a number of reform-minded younger judges have started demanding that judicial appointments be made in a more open and flexible manner.

The nomination process for a new supreme court justice in 2003 brought these demands to the surface, and since then, a change can be noticed in the way judicial appointments are made. Previously, the nomination and appointment of a new justice to the supreme court did not attract much attention because the president usually ap-

pointed the person nominated by the chief justice without much issue.[26] In 2003, however, as the retirement of a supreme court justice
was drawing near,[27] a number of citizen groups[28] had already made
public a list of judges whom they would like to see take his seat on
the supreme court. In response to such demands from citizen groups
and the younger judges, the supreme court announced in August
2003 a meeting of a "Consultative Committee for Nomination of
Supreme Court Justice," which included people other than career
judges, such as the president of the Korean Bar Association, the Minister of Justice, and the president of the National Law Professors
Association. The stated purpose was to provide an avenue through
which nonconventional candidates could be nominated or at least be
given a chance at nomination.

At the meeting, however, the committee members were given
only three candidates to consider, all of whom had been selected by
Chief Justice Choi Jong Young and all of whom had risen up the
through court hierarchy according to seniority. The president of the
Korean Bar Association and the Minister of Justice perceived this as
an affront to the idea of widening the scope of potential nominees
and felt that the chief justice was using the Consultative Committee
as mere window dressing for the appointment process. In protest,
they angrily walked out of the meeting. Also, a group of younger
judges began preparing a joint statement criticizing the supreme court
and the chief justice. One reform-minded judge, named Park Si
Hwan, expressed his displeasure and disappointment at the whole

26. According to the constitution, Justices of the Supreme Court are nominated
by the Chief Justice, and then appointed by the President upon confirmation by the
National Assembly. Korean Constitution, Article 104, §2.

27. Supreme Court Justices in Korea are required by law to retire at the age of
sixty-five. The Chief Justice may serve until the age of seventy. Bŏpwŏn Chojik Pŏp
[Court Organization Act] Art. 45.

28. One salient feature of Korean politics since the 1987 democratic transition
has been the exponential growth in number and variety of citizen groups.

process by turning in his resignation.[29] Furthermore, the president's office made public its displeasure with the actions of the chief justice.

Fearing that this would escalate into a public defiance of the supreme court's authority by the judiciary's own members, the court convened for the first time in history a "Meeting of the Nation's Judges" in order to diffuse tension and to placate the younger judges. Although the meeting may be lauded as a judicial version of participatory democracy, it nevertheless failed to produce a resolution to what was turning into an ideological confrontation between conservative and progressive judges. Yet within days, the so-called judicial crisis was over when the younger, progressive judges backed down, accepting the promise made by Chief Justice Choi that the next appointment process will be more accommodating of their demands.

Indeed, in 2004, when the next vacancy came up, the slot was filled with the first woman justice in the history of Korea, Kim Young Ran, who was also much younger than the class of judges who would have been considered next-in-line for appointment to the supreme court. Once again, prior to the appointment, a number of citizen groups had publicized their own lists of people who they wished would be appointed, and fortunately, the eventual appointee was one of the favorites of the citizen groups. The media and public also welcomed the appointment as a sign that the conservative judiciary is reforming itself by breaking with seniority and promoting diversity among its own members. This trend continued in 2005, when a new chief justice was appointed by President Roh Moo Hyun, and three more justices were appointed by the new chief justice. Particularly, two of the three new justices were greeted by many as likely to contribute to the diversification of the range of viewpoints represented on the bench, as they were generally seen as being relatively more liberal in their judicial philosophy. One of them was Park Si Hwan,

29. This judge was in fact one of the handful of "progressive" judges who had been recommended by citizen groups as a suitable replacement for the retiring Justice.

the judge mentioned above who in 2003 had resigned in protest of the supreme court's lukewarm attitude toward opening up the process of appointment.

In countries like the United States, judicial appointment is often a highly political and politicized process.[30] By comparison, in Korea, until now, judges were seen as relatively apolitical in that they acted like and were perceived to be like career bureaucrats. Although the appointment of a justice of the supreme court did have a political dimension in that both the president and the National Assembly had to be involved in the process, this too did not receive much attention from the people or the media until recently. Perhaps it is a sign of democratization that judicial appointments are becoming a political issue.

For example, the 2005 appointment of the new chief justice, Lee Young Hun, became a political issue when many criticized the president's choice on several counts. First of all, it drew criticism from political opponents of Roh Moo Hyun, who claimed that Roh was merely using the appointment to repay a personal debt—the appointee had served as one of Roh's defense attorneys during the impeachment crisis. Environmentalists and other citizen groups were vehemently opposed to his appointment because he had once represented a developer who intended to build a golf course on the slopes of a mountain surrounding a temple that housed the Tripitaka Koreana.[31] Others expressed concern that he would be too liberal. Dur-

30. In the U.S., the 1987 nomination, and the eventual rejection by the Senate, of Robert Bork as a Supreme Court Justice is perhaps the best-known example of the politicized nature of the appointment process. The more recent politicking over the nomination of Harriet Miers to the highest court and her subsequent withdrawal of her candidacy, as well as the controversy over the confirmation of Samuel Alito, are all reflections of this understanding that judicial appointments are essentially political affairs.

31. Tripitaka Koreana is a national treasure which consists of eighty thousand woodblocks carved in the thirteenth century for printing the entire corpus of all known Buddhist scriptures. It was designated by the UNESCO in 1995 as one of world cultural heritage.

ing his earlier career as a judge, Lee had been known for being lenient in his sentencing, especially in cases in which defendants were charged with having endangered national security. Indeed, after he was sworn in, he initiated a number of reforms aimed at liberalizing and democratizing the judiciary. One is the participation of laypeople in court proceedings mentioned above. Another is a probe into the past wrongdoings of the judiciary, in which the courts acted as the enforcer of the political will of military dictators. He suggested that ways should be found to grant such cases a rehearing.

Although no one disputes the principle that diverse viewpoints and interests should be represented on the supreme court, some activities of the citizen groups are being perceived as a threat to judicial independence. For those accustomed to the old ways, the opinions of these groups are having far too much influence on the appointment process. Some judges are openly complaining that whereas in the past "judicial independence" referred primarily to independence from the executive branch, particularly the president, it has now come to mean independence from certain citizen groups. It may be true that the supreme court has yielded to the demands of the people by appointing candidates favored by those groups, but it would be overstating the case to say that they are dictating the appointment process. In a democratic polity, it is natural for citizens to care about who gets to decide legal cases, especially those with broader social implications. The more critical question that needs to be dealt with is whether such lobbying by citizen groups during appointment processes is incompatible with the ideal of rule of law. Put differently, it must be asked whether this form of people's participation strikes at the core values of constitutionalism.

In some respects, the appointment of justices of the Constitutional Court may have a greater impact on the society because the issues litigated therein are likely to be ones that deal with the fundamentals of the constitutional order. We might say, then, that these appointments should receive greater attention by the people. In that

connection, one by-product of the court's decision on the capital relocation case has been the demand made by supporters of Roh Moo
Hyun that the next vacancy on the court should be filled with someone who shares the political viewpoints of the president. With the
increasing realization that rule of law and the supremacy of the constitution will not always produce the results they desire, they are
demanding that the composition of the court be changed so that there
will be a majority of "reform-minded" justices.

In fact, changes in the composition of the Constitutional Court
have been taking place since 2003. The first woman justice on the
Constitutional Court, Jeon Hyo Sook, was appointed in 2003, even
before the appointment of a woman supreme court justice.[32] She was
appointed to the Constitutional Court by the former Chief Justice
Choi (of the supreme court) shortly after the incident, mentioned
above, in which citizen groups and some younger judges expressed
their disapproval of the conventional manner of making judicial appointments. In that regard, the voice of the people may have had
some bearing on her appointment. And although many people ap-
plauded her appointment as an effort to have more diverse viewpoints
represented on the Constitutional Court, others expressed concern
that Jeon was a classmate of President Roh in the national bar exam.
Was the chief justice bowing to outside pressure by appointing someone who would not disagree with the president's policies? The fact
that she authored the sole dissenting opinion in the capital relocation
case has been interpreted by many as a sign that her views are "progressive," or at least that she holds views more in line with that of
the Roh administration.

In 2005, two more justices were appointed to the Constitutional
Court. One of them, Cho Dae Hyeon, was another lawyer/former
judge who had been a member of Roh Moo Hyun's defense team

---

32. On the appointment process for Constitutional Court Justices, see footnote
5, above.

during his impeachment proceedings. Another classmate of Roh in the national bar exam, Cho was also an attorney representing the government during the capital relocation case. This was obviously a partisan appointment, and it was understood as such because this was a slot for which the ruling party designates the occupant. Moreover, as an appointment that coincided with the wishes of the citizen groups, it may be seen as the beginning of people's increased influence over the appointment of Constitutional Court justices.

Of course, the twist is that President Roh and the citizen groups that are vocal about judicial appointments shared the same agenda of increasing people's participation in all affairs of the government. By the time Roh leaves office, all of the Constitutional Court justices would be appointed during his tenure, either by him directly, by the chief justice he has chosen, or by the National Assembly.[33] Similarly, all but one of the 14 supreme court justices would start their terms under President Roh. Not surprisingly, this caused concern among professional judges that with each appointment of a new justice, the process would become increasingly politicized and judges would inevitably feel the pressure to cater to the demands of a particular group with particular viewpoints. Again, the concern is that judicial independence would suffer, and with it, the rule of law.[34]

---

33. Three of them have already been appointed under President Roh, as mentioned, and all remaining six are due to retire in 2006 and 2007, before the next presidential election.

34. Of course, the ultimate way in which people's opinion can be reflected in the appointment of judges is to hold popular elections. Then, the candidate with the most votes will be appointed as a judge. While such systems do exist in some parts of the world, this risks turning judicial appointments into popularity contests. Even the most progressive citizen groups in Korea have not proposed this system, although it may just be a matter of time before the idea gets floated and starts receiving support. For now, if we are to speculate on why this has not been seriously considered, it may be that the idea brings into stark relief the tension between people's participation and professionalism. Before such system is adopted, people would have to think hard about how to balance the demands for democratic participation and the ideal of rule of law.

## Conclusion

It is perhaps inevitable that with the progress of democracy in Korea, the latent tension between constitutionalism and democracy is becoming more apparent. The ideal of rule of law, therefore, is having a hard time finding its proper place in the pantheon of political values in Korean society. During the period of authoritarian rule, the same people who were demanding more democracy were also arguing for the implementation of rule of law. As tools invoked against oppressive governments, both could be spoken in the same breath without any sense of inconsistency. Yet in the era of democracy after democratization, when everything seemingly must be justified in the name of democracy, any value or institution that has the tendency to restrain democracy is bound to be regarded with suspicion. That is why the idea of allowing unelected justices to overturn policy decisions made by the National Assembly or the president is increasingly receiving criticism.

One way of resolving this problem, at least in theory, may be to adopt a system of government with parliamentary sovereignty. In its ideal form, the concept of parliamentary sovereignty is almost incompatible with the idea of constitutional review, either by a constitutional court or by the regular judiciary. As the branch that embodies the will of the people, the parliament occupies a normatively higher position than either the judiciary or the executive, which are essentially enforcers of the popular will. That is why countries like the United Kingdom until very recently did not have a system of constitutional review. Similarly, in France the ideal of parliamentary sovereignty dictated that the French version of a constitutional court, the *conseil constitutionelle*, be structured as essentially a part of the legislature that can only review legislative proposals before they are enacted and only in an abstract manner (i.e., unrelated to a specific dispute).

Indeed, if Korea is serious about implementing participatory democracy and giving people full control over every aspect of political life, then changing the government system via a constitutional revision to a parliamentary system would be the logical conclusion. This, however, would be a major undertaking with many problems of its own. First of all, the task of revising the constitution is by no means an easy one. Like most constitutions of the world, Korea's constitution is written so that changes cannot be made lightly.[35] More important, even if sufficient political support can be garnered to revise the constitution, it is not at all clear that adopting a parliamentary system will solve the problem. If lessons can be drawn from the recent experiences of other countries, then an important one would be that most governments that used to profess parliamentary sovereignty are now mitigating that claim by introducing in one form or another a system of constitutional review.[36] Most countries of Eastern and Central Europe, where the tradition of parliamentary sovereignty had been relatively strong, have established a constitutional court as part of their democratization process in order to entrench and stabilize democratic politics. Even France and the United Kingdom are moving in the direction of strengthening the agencies in charge of reviewing the constitutionality of legislative and executive actions. In other words,

---

35. It bears noting that proposals for revising the constitution have been made recently by a number of politicians and scholars, but the focus of their arguments does not seems to be on changing the government into a parliamentary system, but rather on other issues such as synchronizing the election cycles of the presidential election and general elections for the National Assembly or allowing the president to serve a second term. Others also argue that we need to revisit the provision that proclaims the entire Korean peninsula as the territory of (South) Korea, in light of the improved relations with North Korea and in recognition of the reality of world politics. Seo Dong-shin, "PM Wants Constitutional Change," *Korea Times*, Jan. 2, 2006; Lee Jin-woo, "Constitutional Reform Should Be Discussed in 2007," *Korea Times*, Oct. 24, 2005.

36. John Ferejohn and Pasquale Pasquino, "Rule of Democracy and Rule of Law," in *Democracy and the Rule of Law*, Jose Maria Maravall and Adam Przeworski eds. (Cambridge: Cambridge University Press, 2003), pp. 242–260.

parliamentary sovereignty regimes are incorporating elements that were developed in the context of a separation-of-powers model of government.

In a government system in which separation of powers is the overriding principle, it is widely understood that the several branches of government are co-equal in status and that their role is to check and restrain one another. This means that even the parliament (or legislature) and the president are not supreme and that they must be kept in check. The principle that comes into play here is the rule of law, and the agency that is entrusted with this task is the judiciary. In other words, in a system of checks and balances, the political branches of the government, which derive their legitimacy from the people, are expected to be cabined and held back by a relatively less democratic branch operating under a principle other than democracy. As Tocqueville noted long ago, a democracy will be more robust if the system is deliberately designed in a way that is not entirely dem-ocratic.[37] By transforming even the most political of problems into legal issues, the system is thereby able to prevent the divisive and fractious tendencies within democratic politics from undermining the very existence of the polity itself. For Tocqueville, this is precisely why as democracy becomes a more entrenched and widely shared value, the principle of rule of law must be strengthened accordingly.[38]

Seen in this light, that the Constitutional Court is playing an increasingly important role in the political life of Koreans can be understood as a natural outcome of the progress of democracy itself. To be sure, Tocqueville's observations were made in reference to the

37. Referring to the legal profession and the principle of rule of law, Tocqueville calls them the only "aristocratic element" that is not only compatible with but also quite necessary for the continued operation of democratic institutions. Alexis de Tocqueville, *Democracy in America*, trans. George Lawrence & ed. J.P. Mayer (New York: Harper Perennial, 1988), pp. 263–270.

38. In his own words: "I hardly believe that nowadays a republic can hope to survive unless the lawyers' influence over its affairs grows in proportion to the power of the people." Ibid. p. 266.

political and legal system of the United States and therefore may not be directly applicable to the Korean system. Yet for better or for worse, the Korean constitutional system, like that of the United States, is based on the principle of separation of powers rather than parliamentary sovereignty. This was at the basis of the Constitutional Court decision, noted above, that rejected the idea of using the national referendum as a vote of confidence. The idea of checks and balances between the various branches is thus an integral part of the Korean system as well. In other words, the principle of rule of law is already woven into the Korean governmental system, and furthermore, it is becoming more activated as democracy becomes more firmly entrenched in Korean society.

Among political and legal scholars, many have offered theories that endeavor to reconcile the potentially conflicting demands of constitutionalism and democracy. Most of these theories have tried to show how constitutionalism, rather than limiting democracy, actually operates to strengthen and reinforce democracy.[39] They also assume that constitutionalism must be legitimated in terms of democracy. What Tocqueville's observations suggest, on the other hand, is that constitutionalism and rule of law are in fact based on very nondemocratic values, which are nevertheless absolutely necessary even for a democratic polity. This is a hard lesson to swallow for those who believe that nondemocratic values simply have no place in a society after democratization. Yet it must be recalled that the problem of reining in political power, particularly the sovereign, through rule of law predates the advent of democracy and that the same problem continues to demand a solution even after the people have replaced the king as the locus of sovereignty. In other words, rule of law is a much older principle that cannot, and perhaps should not, be ex-

39. See, for example, John H. Ely, *Democracy and Distrust* (Cambridge, Mass.: Harvard University Press, 1980); Stephen Holmes, "Precommitment and the Paradox of Democracy," in *Constitutionalism and Democracy*, ed. Jon Elster & Rune Slagstad (Cambridge: Cambridge University Press, 1988).

plained or justified in terms of democracy. The idea of separation of powers may be understood as an attempt to combine this older principle of rule of law with the more modern legitimating principle of democracy. Rule of law in Korea will become firmly established when its political actors, including the Constitutional Court, accept the fact that their system of government was designed in such a way that the spread of democracy will inevitably and naturally bring about the rise of constitutionalist ideals.

CHAPTER THREE

# The Two Tales of the Korean Presidency: Imperial but Imperiled Presidency

Hoon Jaung

## Introduction

In October 2000, a few months after the historic summit with North Korean leader Kim Jong Il, South Korean president Kim Dae Jung seemed to be at the apex of his long political career. The Norwegian Nobel Committee announced on October 13 President Kim Dae Jung won the Nobel Peace Prize "for his decades-long work for democracy and human rights in South Korea and peace and reconciliation on the Korean peninsula." Indeed, the North–South Korea summit meeting in June 2000 furthered not only reconciliation between the two Koreas, but also Kim Dae Jung's personal career. Although the long-time fighter for South Korean democracy largely bypassed democratic procedures in putting together the North–South Korea summit, the historic meeting was touted enthusiastically at home and abroad.

Only a few years later, however, President Kim Dae Jung saw his cherished achievement ruined by criminal charges against senior aides who had helped him realize his vision for a summit meeting. On March 27, 2003, the National Assembly passed a resolution for an independent counsel to investigate the case of the president's top-level aides sending money clandestinely to North Korea. One year later, on March 29, 2004, the Supreme Court ruled that Park Ji Won and Lee Ki Ho, both former special advisors to President Kim Dae

Jung, and Lee Keun Young, former president of the Korean Industrial Bank, violated the South-North Exchange and Cooperation Act in sending US$450 million to North Korea illegally as compensation for the North-South summit. Although President Kim Dae Jung was not indicted, it was widely believed that he was the chief architect of the Blue House officials' criminal acts.

The case illustrates the paradox of the South Korean presidency. On the one hand, the president seemed to be imperial as he circumvented horizontal and vertical constraints in pursuing his foreign policy goals. When President Kim Dae Jung set up the summit meeting and the Five Agreements on intra-Korea reconciliation, he was not under any serious constraints. The National Assembly passed a supporting resolution for the North-South summit in June 2000 without being informed of the meeting's agenda and background. The legal office within the Blue House never had a chance to review the constitutionality and legal grounds of the meeting or the Five Agreements. The government disclosed its plan for the summit to the public the day before the general election on April 14, 2000. But the South Korean presidency has not been completely free of checks and balances. Kim Dae Jung was not the only president who was reprimanded for violating laws while in office. Former president Roh Tae Woo was charged with raising a huge slush fund in the wake of the "clean politics campaign" by his successor, Kim Young Sam, in 1994. Kim Young Sam was also reprimanded. Kim Hyun Chol, President Kim Young Sam's son, was charged with having accumulated an enormous slush fund and having exerted inappropriate influence on governmental policy-making in his last year in the Blue House. Furthermore, President Roh Moo Hyun almost lost his job by parliamentary impeachment resolution—the Constitutional Court gave him a reprieve in May 2004.

The puzzle of imperial presidency in South Korean democracy is not as simple as many analysts have assumed. Most extant studies have been concerned with the excessive power of the president and have searched for reform measures to limit and constrain the president's imperial power. Some studies have proposed enhancing the power of checks on the president by the National Assembly, the Constitutional Court, and the Board of Audit and Inspection. Others have insisted on the need to decentralize presidential power by giving more discretion and power to the prime minister. Yet the 20-year history of South Korean democracy has shown that South Korean presidents have two conflicting features, imperial but imperiled.

This chapter addresses sources and patterns of the two faces of the South Korean presidency in terms of the rule of law. What are the institutional, legal, and cultural sources for an imperial president in this new democracy? How does the imperial president outwit democratic procedures and agents of checks and balances? At the same time, why and how is the once-imperial president constrained by the rule of law? What are the political and institutional factors that make the president accountable to the rule of law? And finally, which reform measures would enhance presidential accountability of the imperial president as well as the imperiled president.

In addressing the two faces of presidency in South Korea, we will focus on the case of Kim Dae Jung's North-South summit meeting and consequent charge of illegally sending money. It represents a recent prominent case of foreign policy issues that reveals the structure and nature of the various dimensions of an imperial but imperiled presidency.

## The Imperial Presidency in South Korea

### Legal Culture in the Blue House:
### A Court of Presidential Authority Without Rule of Law

It is well-known that the South Korean president has predominated the foreign policy–making process, commanding over the bureaucracy, the National Assembly, and civil society.[1] The perception, pri-

1. Lee, Jung-Hoon and Jin Park, "Presidency and Foreign Policy Making in

orities, and leadership style of the president dominates the process and content of foreign policy–making. In this vein, the legal culture and institutional arrangement within the Blue House, the presidential office, is a primary source of the imperial presidency.

A prominent feature of the Blue House is the malfunctioning of institutional apparatus in checking the legal grounds of policy-making decisions by the president and his staff. The executive office of the president includes a legal advisor who is supposed to review the legal grounds of decisions made within the Blue House. Although presidents often select high-ranking public prosecutors for the job, legal advisors have failed in serving as effective legal gatekeepers. Rather than checking the legal grounds of the executive office's decisions, the legal advisor primarily works as a link between the president and the Department of Justice and oversees the president's family members and friends so as to prevent their involvement in corruption scandals.[2]

The failure of the legal advisor results by and large from the president himself. It has been the president who determines the jurisdiction, political power, and duties of senior advisors within the Blue House. In this sense, the restricted role of the legal advisor is closely related to the notion of rule of law of the president. Although Kim Dae Jung has been touted as a crusader for South Korean democratization, he did not seem to appreciate the value of the rule of law, a crucial underpinning of democracy. Although there has been no systematic study about the notion of rule of law as it relates to the South Korean presidency, there are a few clues to the problematic notion of rule of law of the president. Kim Dae Jung's fight for democracy in the last three decades has often relied upon extra-legal,

---

South Korea," paper prepared for Conference on Domestic Determinants of Foreign Policy in South Korea organized by Yonsei University and Asia Foundation, June 14, 2000, Seoul.

2. Interview with Jang, Seong-Min, former advisor to President Kim Dae-jung. July 6, 2004.

unconventional means. Paradoxically, such struggle for democracy did not promote his perception about the value of democratic rules and procedures. On the contrary, he might have developed the notion that the cause of a historic mission would justify a multitude of strategies and devices, whether legal or not, during the course of the democratization movement.

In the case of the North–South Korea summit, Kim Dae Jung revealed his inclination for achieving a historic mission regardless of rule of law. In February 2003, the final month of his tenure, faced with growing pressure to explain secretly sending money to the North, President Kim Dae Jung defended the action by emphasizing historical cause and the impact of the summit. He stated that "although there are some faults in putting together the summit meeting, I believe history will evaluate the summit's contribution to the reconciliation of the two Koreas and laying the groundwork for peaceful reunification. For the groundwork of reunification, some efforts had to be pursued in secret and at times beyond legal framework."[3] In other words, he asserted that the North-South summit was a case of "political question" of national interest that are beyond a judicial review of constitutionality.

Another crucial factor responsible for an imperial presidency was the decision-making structure within the Blue House. The royal-court model explains better than other alternatives what was happening in Kim Dae Jung's Blue House. Like his predecessors, President Kim Dae Jung was a reigning monarch and the Blue House was his court, especially in the foreign policy–making arena. Decision-making power was highly centralized in a monarchical manner. The president's beliefs and worldviews predominated foreign policy–making. The so-called Sunshine Policy, the reconciliation policy, is a prime case. Senior advisors were merely courtiers who were subject to the whims of

3. Chosun Ilbo, Feb. 13, 2003. p.1.

the president and simply carried out the presidential decisions.[4] Only when one stuck to presidential beliefs with unwavering loyalty could one sustain one's power within the inner circle of foreign policy decision making.

In President Kim Dae Jung's court of the Blue House, there was a race for the president's favor among key advisors and senior aides. In this heated race, the crucial factor was neither policy expertise nor experience, but loyal dedication to the philosophy of the three-stage reunification model of Kim Dae Jung.[5] It was why Park Ji Won, special advisor to the president without portfolio, a classic courtier, won the power struggle within the Blue House. It was not the Minister of Reunification, but Park Ji Won, along with National Intelligence Service Director, Lim Dong Won, who practically led the meetings with the North in preparation for the summit meeting. Within this blind race for power, legal procedures and relevant laws were often neglected. Indeed, the Minister of Reunification, Park Jay Gyu, who was in charge of the North-South relationship, was virtually excluded in the summit preparation meetings that was going on in early 2000 in Shanghai, Beijing, and Singapore. He came to know about the summit only a few days before the government made its schedule public.[6]

The rule of law was confronted with a crucial test when the North asked the Blue House to secretly send US$ 500 million as a final condition for participation in the April 2000 summit. Faced with this

---

4. Kohl, Wilfred, "The Nixon-Kissinger Foreign Policy System and US-European Relations: Patterns of Policy Making," *World Politics* 28, no. 1: 3.

5. For the concepts and evolution of Kim Dae-jung's reunification model, see Moon, Chung-In and David Steinberg, eds. *Kim Dae-jung Government and Sunshine Policy: Promises and Challenges.* Seoul: Yonsei University Press, 1999. For the role of personal beliefs and world system on Kim Dae-jung's Sunshine policy, see Kim, Jeong-Yong, *South Korea's Sunshine Policy, 1998-2002: Domestic Imperatives and Private Interests.* Unpublished dissertation. University of Warwick, 2002.

6. Lee, Kyokwan, *The Dangerous Deal of Kim Dae-jung Administration,* Seoul: Hansong, 2002.

impudent demand from the North, senior advisors to President Kim
Dae Jung were divided. Lee Ki Ho, economic advisor to the president,
opposed the action, pointing to the legal problems. He asserted that
such money had to be sent in the form of a South-North Cooperation
Fund, which required parliamentary approval. But Lee was sur-
rounded by loyal courtiers who were willing to violate relevant laws
for the sake of a historic cause, so he reluctantly went along with
pushing the Hyundai conglomerate and the Korea Development Bank
to raise and send money to the North.[7] In other words, the court
politics among the president and his senior advisors put more value
on the so-called historic cause of pursuing a summit than on observing relevant laws.

### Lack of Horizontal Checks

When Arthur Schlesinger coined the term "imperial presidency," he
talked about the lack of basic horizontal checks, particularly in the
congress, on presidential decision making in the foreign policy arena.[8]
The historian pointed to the rise of an imperial presidency in the
United States, a presidential system with a highly powerful legislature. Thus, he reasoned, it is no wonder that new democracies with
presidential system are likely to suffer from symptoms of an imperial
presidency. Most new democracies have inherited an authoritarian
legacy that often comprises the tradition of a strong executive branch
and a feeble legislature. South Korea has been no exception to this
pattern.

In the case of the 2000 summit and the secret sending of money,
South Korean National Assembly did not exert proper constraining
power on decision making in the Blue House. The National Assembly, in particular the Reunification and Foreign Relations Committee,
did not know about the preparations for the summit, which had been

7. *Report of Song Doo Whan Independent Counsel.*
8. Schlesinger, Arthur, *The Imperial Presidency*, New York: Houghton Mifflin,
1973.

going on for a few months in early 2000. Most members of the National Assembly learned of the meeting only when the government revealed its plan for the summit, which was on April 14, 2000, the day before the general election. Also, the National Assembly was not informed of the agenda of the two leaders' meeting, which included some breakthroughs in the North-South relationship. The June 15 summit declared Five Agreements between the two Koreas with regard to the principle of reunification and reconciliation. And as there was no information-sharing between the two branches of governments, the National Assembly did not learn about the secret cooperation fund as a condition for the summit meeting.

All the National Assembly did was to give political support for the summit without close investigation into the summit's process, agenda, and related illegal fund. The Reunification and Foreign Relations Committee passed a resolution that supported the cause of the summit on June 9, 2000, six days before it was scheduled to take place. After the summit, June 20 and 21, the committee held a special session to discuss the Five Agreements reached in the summit. But even though the majority of the committee members expressed concern over and opposition to the Five Agreements, they could not revoke the accord of the leaders of the North and South. In sum, the National Assembly neither constrained the fiscal issues in the summit nor exerted oversight on an agenda that was to have huge implications for the future of the intra-Korea relationship.

Institutional and political factors were responsible for the lack of horizontal constraints from the National Assembly. Although there have been high expectations for an active role of the National Assembly since the democratic transition in 1987, such expectations have been largely betrayed.[9] The National Assembly continues to suffer from various institutional and behavioral drawbacks and legacies from

9. Shin, Doh C. *Mass Politics and Culture in Democratizing Korea.* New York: Cambridge University Press, 1999: 147.

Table 1. Legislation in the 16th National Assembly

| | Total of 16 Standing Committees | | | | Reunification and Foreign Affairs Committee | | | |
|---|---|---|---|---|---|---|---|---|
| | Pro-posed | Pass | Reject | Dis-carded | Pro-posed | Pass | Reject | Dis-carded |
| Total Number of Bills | 3,025 | 1,381 | 16 | 1,583 | 52 | 26 | 0 | 26 |
| Bill of Acts | 2,507 | 948 | 4 | 1,514 | 15 | 3 | 0 | 12 |
| Member Bill | 1,912 | 517 | 3 | 1,351 | 12 | 0 | 0 | 12 |
| Gov't Bill | 595 | 431 | 1 | 163 | 3 | 3 | 0 | 0 |
| Approval for General Session | 235 | 204 | 11 | 17 | 37 | 17 | 0 | 12 |
| Resolution for General Session | | 283 | 229 | 1 | 52 | | 6 | |

the authoritarian past. The verdict on the performance of the National Assembly has not been overly positive. It has been seen as an immature legislative body, suffering from limited institutional autonomy, playing only a marginal role in lawmaking, and being plagued by partisan gridlock and distorted representation.[10]

In the context of a frail National Assembly in democratic South Korea, lawmaking and legislative oversight in the area of foreign policy has been particularly problematic. In Table 1, data about the lawmaking pattern in 16 standing committees and the Reunification and Foreign Affairs Committee (RFAC) show that lawmaking in the foreign policy arena has been especially meager. The RFAC has handled only 4.3 percent of the bills processed in the 16th National Assembly. This figure is alarming, as there are 16 standing committee in the legislative body. Furthermore, a majority (80 percent) of the bills that went to the RFAC were either resolutions or approval bills. Most striking in Table 1 is the number of member bills that were passed

10. Park, Chan-Wook, "Legislative-Executive Relations and Legislative Reform," in Diamond, Larry and Doh C. Shin, eds. *Institutional Reform and Democratic Consolidation in Korea*, Stanford, Calif.: Hoover Institution Press, 2000.

Table 2. Number of Sessions in the 16th National Assembly

| | |
|---|---|
| Total of Standing Committees | 922 |
| Reunification and Foreign Affairs Committee | 52 |

Source: *Report of Reunification and Foreign Affairs Committee*, National Assembly, 2004.

in the 16th National Assembly. The National Assemblymen in this committee had proposed just 19 member bills and only one of them was passed in their four-year term.

Various institutional and political barriers have kept the National Assembly—in particular the RFAC, the workshop forum in parliamentary foreign policy–making—from holding the president accountable for policy decisions while investigating possible irregularities, policy failures, and abuses of power. Most of all, the rules of the RFAC are responsible for scanty constraints. The RFAC, like other standing committees, needs the approval of the majority party of the committee membership when it initiates legislative investigation, including summoning witnesses and sending for documentation. That is, a minority party is not able to initiate any legislative investigation by itself.

In addition, organizational and behavioral patterns in the RFAC are also sources of limited constraining capacity. Like other standing committees, the RFAC maintains a very limited legislative staff, only six full-time legislative assistants plus secretarial assistants. Lacking versions of the American Congressional Research Service and Governmental Accounting Office, this tiny staff helps committee members oversee policy activities and budgets of the Ministry of Reunification (580 billion won for the 2005 budget, staff of 436 and the Ministry of Foreign Affairs and Trade (775.5 billion won for the 2005 budget, staff of 1,925). Furthermore, the composition and culture of the RFAC have hampered effective oversight on foreign policy–making. For a long time, the RFAC has been regarded as a highly privileged, unofficial "senate," and party leaders and senior members from political parties have constituted most of the committee membership. In the 16th National Assembly RFAC, there were only two first-term Assemblymen; the other members were in their third or fourth term in the RFAC. The paradox of the unofficial senate is that party leaders and senior members spend most of their time and efforts on intra-party affairs rather than on legislative activities.[11]

### Legitimacy of the Relevant Laws

When the supreme court found a few senior aides to President Kim Dae Jung guilty of violating the South-North Korea Exchange and Cooperation Act in March 2004, there was no frenzied reaction to the verdict among the public. The court's ruling said that those aides committed criminal acts by not seeking parliamentary approval and not obtaining approval from the Ministry of Reunification when they sent US$450 million to North Korea.

Although the verdict was not questioned, the case raised issues in implementing rule of law in the inter-Korea relationship. It high-lighted two crucial loopholes in the current relevant laws. On the one hand, the independence and fairness of law enforcement was not as high as was widely believed. When there was a growing interest in the case on the part of the public and the media, the Department of Justice held over the investigation, quoting the need for parliamentary investigation ahead of legal investigation. As the President had vir-tually monopolized the appointment power of most high-ranking pros-ecutors, the Department of Justice was a far cry from being politically independent. As we will see later, the case was investigated by in-dependent counsel appointed by the opposition-controlled National Assembly.

11. An empirical study finds out that South Korean parliamentary members tend to spend less time and effort for legislative activities, as the number of their terms extends. Sohn, Byung-Kwon, "Legislative Activities: An Evaluation of Standing Com-mittee Activities," paper presented at the Fiftieth Anniversary Conference of the Korean National Assembly. May 22–3, 1998. (in Korean)

A more severe and subtle issue had to do with the legitimacy of relevant laws in the intra-Korea relationship. The foremost issue, about the legitimacy of relevant law, is related to clear and definite prescription. There are two major acts that regulate the intra-Korea relationship: the South-North Korea Exchange and Cooperation Act (SNECA) and the South-North Korea Cooperation Fund Act (SNCFA). First, the SNECA does not provide effective specifics about modes, actors, and the legality of exchange and cooperation between the two Koreas. For instance, it prescribes that intra-Korea cooperation can take the form of either trade or nontrade exchanges, but does this so vaguely that it has to regulate every possible form of contact and exchange.[12]

Second, the SNECA has contained some prescription in conflict with extant law, in particular the National Security Law. Whereas the SNECA regulates contacts with and visits to North Korea for reconciliation between the two Koreas, the National Security Law prohibits infiltration into and exit from North Korea. The distinction between reconciliatory contacts and conspiring infiltration is based upon whether such behaviors defend liberal democracy. As the distinction relies upon a highly vague and abstract line, there is ample room for arbitrary implementation of the relevant laws. For instance, when a South Korean nongovernmental organization (NGO) makes contact with a North Korean NGO on the issue of food aid, it can be labeled either a lawful cooperation or an illegal infiltration by the arbiter of prosecutors.[13]

In addition, the distinctions and conflicts between the SNECA and SNCFA bring an old controversy to the fore: the heated confrontation between those who support and those who oppose the National Security Law. Since the democratic transition in 1987, there

12. Je, Seong-Ho, *Legal Issues in North-South Korea Economic Exchanges*. Seoul: Jimmundang, 2003: 88 (in Korean).

13. Jong, Tae-Wook, "National Security Law and Peace in Korean Peninsular," *Democratic Legal Studies* 16 (1999): 47–57 (in Korean).

have been various attempts to eliminate the National Security Law, which had been often abused to oppress political dissidents during the authoritarian era. Liberal reunification movement activists made visits to North Korea without governmental permission in order to invalidate and demonstrate the ineffectiveness of the National Security Law. Prominent among those were novelist Hwang Seokyong, the reverend Moon Ikwan, and college student Lim Sukyung. Also, several NGOs emerged that advocated the elimination of the National Security Law. In 2000, 232 progressive NGOs launched a nationwide network to eradicate the law. The network expanded, comprising 305 NGOs in 2004.[14]

In a nutshell, the relevant laws do not seem to provide an effective framework for regulating and facilitating the intra-Korea relationship. The scanty SNECA and SNCFA have failed in laying legal ground for the rapidly evolving relationship between the two Koreas. The legitimacy of the old National Security Act has been undermined drastically in recent years. As a result, implementing rule of law in the field of intra-Korea relations becomes highly chaotic and demanding.

With regard to the power of an imperial presidency, the case of the illegal cooperation fund has not reduced the twilight zone between granted authority and implicitly delegated power of the president in the intra-Korea relationship. Given the limited specification and restrained legitimacy of the current relevant laws, President Kim Dae Jung was stating a partial truth when he asserted that the case was beyond the current jurisdiction system. Yet the vague criterion of historic cause does not guarantee the transparency and fairness of the rule of law. Inevitably, it calls for a new law regulating the scope and power of presidential authority in dealing with intra-Korea issues, like the presidential War Powers Act in the United States.

14. As the liberal party, the Uri Party, has obtained the majority of the National Assembly in the April 2004 election, it has been trying to abolish the National Security Act and to revamp relevant articles in other criminal acts.

## The Other Side of the Story:
## The Imperial President Under Siege

The imperial presidents in South Korea have not been invincible at all. Although they are successful in belittling vertical and horizontal checks on their power most of the time, they are not completely untouchable. South Korean presidents are occasionally subject to constraints from the National Assembly, the public, the media, and civic associations. Furthermore, every president since the democratic transition in 1987 has been punished, directly or indirectly, for violating laws. In other words, constraining the imperial president has been working occasionally. In this sense, South Korean democracy has made tangible, if not remarkable, progress in restraining the imperial president.

### Preconditions of Circumscribing the Presidency:
### From Imperial to Lame-Duck President

The foremost condition for restraining an imperial president has to do with the level of political resources of the president. As long as the president maintains abundant political resources, he seems to be beyond vertical and horizontal constraints. A significant component of presidential political resources lies with his popularity among the public. It is hard for opposition party members, the media, and presidential aides and staff to constrain a president who has high public approval. For instance, when President Kim Young Sam enjoyed unusually high level of popularity, about 90 percent, with his audacious drive for political reform in his early months in office in 1993, it was very difficult to criticize abuse of presidential authorities and review the legality of his reform drive. In this vein, when President Kim Dae Jung recovered his once-flagging public support, reaching the sound level of 60 percent after the historic summit in June 2000, there was no serious challenge with regard to the legality of the preparation process and the constitutionality of the Five Agreements made during the summit meeting.

American students of the presidency have argued that presidential popularity relies upon electoral mandate, presidential performance (in particular, economic performance), national crisis, and the like.[15] For South Korean presidents, political performance rather than economic performance stands salient in shaping popularity among the public. Whereas good economic conditions tend to help many presidents garner public approval to a certain extent, the South Korean public has been much more sensitive to political performance, especially corruption around the president.[16] For example, inheriting an International Monetary Fund conditionality economy in 1998, President Kim Dae Jung had to struggle with a malingering economy in his early years in office. Despite the flagging economy, his public approval rate was remarkably high, 60 to 70 percent, in 1998. Yet the approval rate began to plummet rapidly when the president's spouse was revealed to have allegedly been involved in a bribery scandal among wives of ministers, the so-called fur-gate, in 1999. Also, President Kim Young Sam, who commanded over 90 percent public approval rate in his first year in office, lost most of his political resources when his son, Kim Young Chol, the closest advisor of the president, was charged with involvement in a huge slush fund scandal in 2002.

Another key factor in presidential political resources is related to the temporal cycle of presidential tenure and the election cycle. As the South Korean constitution allows only one term for the president, most presidents inevitably suffer from the lame-duck phenomenon toward the later phase of their tenure. One dimension of a lame-duck president is steady decline of public approval throughout presidential

15. For instance, see Brody, Richard, *Assessing the President: The Media, Elite Opinion, and Public Support*. Stanford: Stanford University Press, 1991.

16. For more about the dynamics of popular support for South Korean presidents, see Jaung, Hoon, "Politics, Economy, and Dynamics of Presidential Popularity in the Kim Dae-jung Government in South Korea, *Journal of East Asian Studies* 2, no. 1: 241–259.

tenure. Although there can be a few exceptional ups and downs, South Korean presidents have experienced a simple pattern of popularity movement. Presidents tend to have high level of support from the public early in their tenure, then the support begins to decline steadily after 18 months in office. Toward the end of their tenure, most presidents suffer from a dismal level of public support (12 to 15 percent for Kim Young Sam, Kim Dae Jung and Roh Tae Woo).

Amid declining public approval toward the end of tenure, the president also gradually loses his authority over the bureaucracy, his own party members, and the cabinet. As the president exhausts his power of appointing key posts in the cabinet, bureaucratic organizations, public companies, and others, his authority begins to ebb remarkably. A most notable case has to do with presidential power for party nomination for parliamentary election. As a charismatic leader of a highly personalized party, the South Korean president has dominated the power of nomination for parliamentary candidates.[17] But once the president uses up his power of nomination for parliamentary election, he loses his control over his own party and slips into a lame-duck presidency. To make matters worse, due to the nonconcurrent election cycle between the legislative (four-year term) and the presidential election (five-year term), most presidents have gone through legislative election in the middle of presidential tenure.

In a nutshell, like his predecessors, president Kim Dae Jung was no longer an imperial president in late 2002 when opposition party member Eum Ho Sung first raised the issue of the secret cooperation fund for the summit during a parliamentary investigation session on September 25, 2002. The president's popularity had dropped to about

17. Presidential leadership over personalized party has abruptly broken down in the later year of Kim Dae-jung government, as the governing party, the New Millenium Democratic Party has decentralized party organization as well as nomination process for parliamentary and presidential candidates in late 2001. See Hoon Jaung," Seen Goals and Unseen Effects: Reform of Presidential Primaries and Changing dynamics of Party Politics in South Korea and US," *Journal of Korean Legislative Studies* 8, no. 2: 178–206 (2002) (in Korean).

15 percent, and his authority was further severely tainted by a slush fund scandal involving his own sons.

### Bashing the Lame-Duck President: A Way of Rule of Law?

When the president turns from imperial to lame-duck toward the end of his tenure, conditions are ripe to restrain him. But a lame-duck president does not make policy decisions actively, as he has lost most of his political resources. Thus, the paradox is that an imperial president's policymaking is not subject to rule of law with his invincible authority whereas a lame-duck president is not subject to rule of law because he makes few policy-decisions.

As a result, constraining a lame-duck president often focuses on past illegal decision-making or abuse of presidential authority rather than on anything going on in the present. When it becomes clear that the president has become a lame duck, various players participate in unveiling cases of past unlawful acts and abuses of authority by the president and bringing such cases to justice. The first attempt to bash the president in the name of rule of law often comes from opposition parliamentary members or media who happen to gain access to veiled information within the government. Then the issue becomes salient as the media and the public pay increasing attention to the case. Eventually, independent counsel rather than public prosecutors investigate and bring justice.

In the case of the secret cooperation fund, the long road to bring the case to justice was triggered by an opposition parliamentary member. National Assemblyman Eum Ho Seong first raised the issue of the secret fund during the parliamentary oversight session in September 2002, when about 100 days of President Kim Dae Jung's tenure remained. Based upon an unidentified source, the opposition parliamentary member made the allegation that the Hyundai conglomerate and the Korea Development Bank were heavily and illegally involved with the secret cooperation fund under pressure from the Blue House.

Although the allegation drew irritated responses from both the Hyundai conglomerate and the Korea Development Bank, the media gave the case extensive coverage, and it began to snowball. Updates about the case repeatedly hit headlines of leading newspapers and major television news. It developed into a salient political issue in the following months, October 2002 through January 2003, that comprised flurries of investigation reports by media, defenses of those allegedly involved with the case, and growing demand from various civic activist groups for close investigation by law enforcement agencies.[18]

After months of allegations and defenses in the realm of civil society, the issue moved into the realm of governmental jurisdiction as President-elect Roh Moo Hyun (who was elected on December 17, 2002), said on January 18, 2003, that public prosecutors had to look into the case. The president-elect wanted to demonstrate his sensitivity to the public concern with the issue by pressing public prosecutors.

Faced with pressure from both the public and the president-elect, the Board of Audit and Inspection (BAI) and public prosecutors tepidly undertook the investigation into the case in late January 2003. However, the two law enforcement agencies suffered from an innate limitation of their ability to carry out a comprehensive investigation into allegedly illegal acts by the Blue House. Neither the public prosecutors nor the BAI had the proper political independence from the president. The president not only retained the power to appoint the heads of and high-ranking officials in both the BAI and the Justice Department but also had the right to control their budgets.

As a result, the investigations by the BAI and the public prosecutors were no more than nominal and merely saved face. The BAI investigation revealed that there were some irregularities around the load and some favors extended to Hyundai and that the loan was

18. Various issues of *Chosun Daily, Joong-Ang Daily.*

illegally transferred to North Korea from the Korea Development Bank. But the BAI did not take any steps to bring justice to the case. The Justice Department looked even worse when it announced its decision to hold over investigation into the case, citing both the need for parliamentary investigation and the historic cause of reconciliation between North and South Korea. This decision triggered angry reactions from the public, the media, and civic activist groups.

The lukewarm actions by the two law enforcement agencies invited an active role on the part of the National Assembly in unraveling illegal or improper acts of the imperial president. Embarrassed by the inactions of BAI and the Justice Department, the National Assembly passed a resolution to establish an independent counsel to look into the case. Kim Dae Jung's Democratic Party members opposed the resolution, but on February 26, 2003, the opposition Grand National Party passed it with its comfortable majority within the National Assembly.

With the support of public opinion and a well-staffed legal team, the independent counsel, Song Doo Whan, conducted a comprehensive investigation into the case of the secret cooperation fund over 80 days from April to June 2003. The investigation included interrogations of senior officials from the Blue House, members of the National Intelligence Service, and leaders of the Korea Development Bank, and Hyundai. The investigation did not include interrogation of former president Kim Dae Jung. Based upon the indictment by independent counsel, the supreme court found several senior advisors to President Kim Dae Jung and the Korea Development Bank director guilty of having violated the SNECA in March 2004.

In a nutshell, once a South Korean president becomes a lame-duck president in the latter part of his tenure, he looks imperiled, lacking the authority and political means to pursue his own policy goals. Then the president is vulnerable to criticism and law enforcement that penalizes illegal and irregular behaviors committed during his early imperial years. In some sense, such disciplining of the president shows gradual progress of rule of law in this new democracy. It is clearly progress of the accountability of South Korean democracy that an imperial president might face prosecution for illegal acts committed during his tenure. Yet this pattern of imperiled presidency is far from sound improvement in terms of rule of law. Most of all, the current pattern of bashing a lame-duck president focuses on post-facto punishment rather than on prevention. Although Presidents Roh Tae Woo and Kim Young Sam fell victim to post-facto punishment, this did not change a similar pattern of power abuses and violation of law by their successor, President Kim Dae Jung. South Korean presidents apparently do not choose to learn from the mistakes of their predecessors.

## Conclusion

As we have discussed, the South Korean presidency has been Janus-faced: imperial, then imperiled. Such a presidency requires a reform agenda for an effective and accountable president to take a two-track path. On the one hand, it calls for institutional and political reform that enhances accountability of the president to horizontal and vertical checks. On the other hand, there need to be reform measures that curtail the declining competence of a lame-duck president while keeping him accountable.

With regard to reform to constrain an imperial president, there have been extensive debates. Several studies have proposed various institutional reform measures that would make the imperial president accountable. They include institutional reform that strengthens the restraining powers and resources of the National Assembly, the BAI, public prosecutors, and the Constitutional Court. To enhance the constraining role of the National Assembly, studies have proposed reform measures that increase budgets, support staff, and research and information capability and that vitalize the legislative oversight and investigative capacity of the National Assembly.[19] Also, to im-

19. For proposed comprehensive reform measures for the National Assembly, see

prove the political independence of the BAI, it has been suggested that it be transferred to the National Assembly and that the tenure of the director of the BAI needs to be extended and guaranteed. For enhanced independence of public prosecutors from an imperial president, guaranteeing tenure for the attorney general and senior public prosecutors is crucial. In addition, to revitalize the constraining power of the Constitutional Court on an imperial president, the court should have a more active role in reviewing arbitrary decrees by the president and in restraining pardons by the president.[20]

The other dimension of reform has to do with improving the political capacity of a lame-duck president while keeping him in check. Several studies have argued that the nonconcurrent electoral cycle has to be made concurrent. As parliamentary elections (four-year term) and presidential elections (five-year term) are held on a different election calendar, the president is highly likely to become a lame duck after the parliamentary election[21] during his tenure. In relation to this, it has been repeatedly suggested that the South Korean president needs to be allowed to run for second term. As the constitution allows only one term for the president, it is inevitable that a president becomes a lame duck after only two or three years in office.

In addition to institutional reform, legitimacy of relevant law has to be enhanced for more effective rule of law. Such reform has to be pursued along two crucial lines. One is to improve fairness in implementing law enforcement. After over 20 years of democracy, the public still maintains a low estimation of the way that rule of law is

---

Park Chan-Wook, Byung-Kook Kim, and Hoon Jaung eds. *Conditions for the Success of National Assembly*, Seoul: EAI, 2004 (in Korean).

20. Mo, Jongryn, "Reforming Korean Presidency: Toward a Balance of Responsibility and Capacity," paper presented at the Annual Conference of Korean Political Science Association, Daejon, June 24, 2004 (in Korean).

21. Furthermore, president's party tend to lose seats in parliamentary elections held in the middle of president's tenure. Jaung, Hoon "Political Institutional Sources of Instability in Korean Presidential System," *Korean Political Science Review* 35, no. 4: 107–127 (in Korean).

enforced. People believe that law enforcement is lenient or even lethargic when it comes to those who have political influence or veto power. An imperial president is a prime example of one who bypasses law enforcement. Here again, political independence of law enforcement agencies is crucial.

The other is to enhance legitimacy of law by providing effective and comprehensive provisions that regulate presidential decisions. President Kim Dae Jung defended the secret cooperation fund case by citing the political question of national interest for the sake of national reunification and implicitly pointing out the incomprehensiveness of current laws on intra-Korea exchanges and reconciliation. Against this argument, the supreme court ruling stated that current law should be obeyed by the president, and rejected the notion of political question of national interest. It wrote that unless there is urgent need for swift action while lacking means other than following current laws, the president should respect current laws. In this sense, the supreme court decided that the secret cooperation fund did not meet those conditions of exemption from current laws. Thus, the task for the future is to determine how to settle these issues as regards regulating presidential behavior in the arena of foreign policy–making.

# CHAPTER FOUR

# How Does Democracy Reduce Money Politics?: Competition versus the Rule of Law

Jongryn Mo

## Introduction

The 20 years of Korea's democratic experience show that democracy does not come easily. One of the biggest barriers to succeeding as a democracy has been the persistence of money politics. By all reasonable estimates, Korean democracy is one of the most expensive systems to run. In the presidential election of 1997, two major candidates reported that they each spent about US$20 million. Considering that spending limits on a major party candidate in the general election part of the 2002 U.S. presidential contest were US$60 million and the U.S. GDP is about 20 times larger than the Korean GDP, the official figures reported in Korea are not small. But the reality is much worse; it is widely believed that Korean presidential candidates actually spend much more than what they report, sometimes up to ten times more. More worrisome is the pervasiveness of corruption in party and campaign finance. Fair or not, everyone believes that there is not a single politician who does not break the law.

Given the bleak state of money politics in Korea, it may be futile to look for any systematic change in money politics since democracy began in 1987; in everyone's mind, things have remained the same, if not worsened. However, in spite of widespread pessimism and the paucity of objective data, it is important to look back and see whether there has been any change in the way money politics works in Korea. If we do not have an objective view of where we stand at the moment, we will repeat the same mistakes over and over again based on prevailing myths and misconceptions.

Indeed, a careful look into the history of presidential elections over the past 20 years reveals that the type and level of political corruption have significantly changed. One can even see some positive developments in the rise of reform candidates. Understanding how this happened requires some effort to analyze the underlying forces of change in party politics. But the downside is that whatever progress Korea has made so far has not been grounded on a firm institutional foundation. Exogenous change in party competition, not an effective system of regulation, has been the main driving force.

## Concepts and Theories

How do the cost of elections and the level of corruption change? A standard framework in the literature for explaining the pattern and level of corruption is to evaluate the distribution of bargaining power between the payer and taker of a bribe (Rose-Ackerman 1978). In a major study of Korean money politics before and after the democratic transition of 1987, Kang (2002) uses this bargaining approach, positing the state and business as parties to corrupt transactions. Their bargaining power, in turn, is assumed to vary according to their organizational coherence; the key indicators for the bargaining power of business and the state are the number of firms and the unity of the state, respectively.[1]

---

1. The distribution of bargaining power between contributors and politicians has also been a key variable in the study of campaign contributions in the United States because campaign contributions have been understood as a form of investments. Recently, however, a dissenting view has emerged that contributions is a form of political participation with little expectation of money-for-benefit exchange (Ansolabehere, Figueiredo, and Snyder, 2002).

Since Kang's model is developed to compare the type and level of overall corruption before and after a high-growth year, it has to be modified to suit our setting, political corruption in the context of presidential elections under democracy. Two main parties to illegal exchanges of contributions and political favors in my framework are the ruling party and the business sector. I focus on the ruling party because it has been more prone to corruption than an opposition party, accounting for most of the corruption in Korea.

The party's bargaining power relative to corporate donors depends on how much benefit it can potentially deliver to the donors after the election. When the party candidate makes promises to the donors, he will be much more credible if he has the support of the incumbent president, who has the power to give favors before and after the campaign before he leaves office, and if he enjoys a high probability of winning. Thus, the bargaining power of the ruling party will be strong when the ruling party is coherent, that is, there is no conflict between the incumbent president and his candidate, and the candidate is expected to win. In contrast, the bargaining power will be weak if the opposition scenario holds, that is, if its candidate is an underdog or a long shot in the polls and has a strained relationship with the incumbent president.

How much benefit corporate donors expect to derive from their contributions also depends on how dependent their business is on the government. If government intervention in the economy is extensive, a good business-government relationship is an important determinant of corporate success, so the benefit of a given political favor, which is exchanged for contributions, would be large. The opposite is true when the economy is market-oriented. Since corporate success in a competitive market is determined largely by market factors, the benefit of the same political favor would be smaller. As the economy becomes more dependent on the government, the value of a political favor increases for a donor, forcing the donor to make more contri-

Figure 1.  Levels of Illegal Corporate Contributions
          Under Different Types of Political Exchange

| Business | Ruling Party | |
|---|---|---|
| | *Coherent/High Probability of Winning* | *Fractured/Low Probability of Winning* |
| Market-dependent | Type I: Bargaining Medium Amount | Type II: Arms-Length Small Amount |
| Government-dependent | Type III: Predation Large Amount | Type IV: Capture Medium Amount |

butions for the same favor. Thus, a donor's bargaining power is larger
when the economy is more market-oriented.[2]

Depending on the values of these two variables—the political
strength of the ruling party and the economic orientation of the business sector—there can be four analytically distinct types of political
exchange (Figure 1). In the first case, business is politically vulnerable
but economically independent, and the ruling party and business are
expected to bargain on relatively equal footing. By contributing to a
strong ruling party, business wants to make sure that the party will
create or maintain a favorable business environment. But business
would not be willing to contribute large amounts because the influence of the government is limited in a market-oriented economy.

When the ruling party is weak ahead of the election in a market-
oriented economy, business would be very cautious about contributing to the ruling party, and if it doesn't, it would not offer much more
than what it would give to the leading opposition party. In this uncertain environment, business would try to keep every contending
political party at arm's length and hedge its bets by distributing its
funds thinly across parties.[3]

2. Empirical research shows that there is a negative relationship between economic freedom and corruption (Chafuen and Guzman, 2000).

3. This assumes that donors want to buy access or seek political benefits when

The third type of political exchange occurs when a strong ruling party meets a government-dependent business sector. In this case, the ruling party with a preponderance of bargaining power can dictate the terms of exchange to the business. If the ruling party happens to have authoritarian tendencies, it can take the practice to an extreme form of predation. The level of illegal contributions will also be high. Not only can the ruling party demand more money, but also it can raise money separately through the president and the candidate. In an environment in which not even the president and the candidate are perfectly forthcoming to each other about their fund-raising activities, donors are not able to play one against the other; thus, they contribute separately to both of them, sometimes doubling the contribution amounts that they might have given to one recipient.

When a government-dependent business sector faces a weak ruling party, the business sector gets a chance to manage a government-business relationship on its terms. If business is successful in capturing the government after the election on the basis of campaign contributions, it can reap large economic benefits, so it would be willing to donate relatively large amounts of money to the ruling party. But since the ruling party is weak, it may not take much for the business sector to win desired concessions from the ruling party. Thus, the amount of contributions under this type of political exchange will stay in the medium range.

The simple framework of political exchange involving illegal corporate contributions suggests that there are two main routes, regulation and competition, to alleviating the problem of illegal donations (table 1).[4] Regulation discourages illegal donations by increasing the

making political contributions. If, instead, they are ideologically motivated, they may contribute more money to their favored candidates in close elections.

4. Enhancing regulation and competition is consistent with common anti-corruption strategies espoused by international organizations. The World Bank (2000), for example, describes five components of an anti-corruption strategy as institutional restraints, political accountability, civil society participation, competitive private sector, and public sector management. The first three conditions are needed to

Table 1. Alternative Approaches to Campaign Finance Reform

| Approaches | Components | Sub-Models | Conditions for success |
|---|---|---|---|
| Regulation | Rules | Public financing<br>Contribution/spending limits<br>Transparency | Completeness (no loopholes)<br>Enforceability<br>Regulatory authority<br>Adequate penalties and sanctions<br>Compatibility with local conditions<br>Fairness |
| | Enforcement | | Independent regulators<br>Independent prosecution/judiciary<br>Party reform<br>Civil society participation |
| Competition | Political competition | | Democracy<br>Electoral competitiveness<br>Reform voters |
| | Economic competition | | Deregulation/privatization<br>Administrative reform<br>Openness to trade and investment<br>Strong corporate governance<br>Financial transparency |

expected cost of violations (the size of punishment times the probability of getting caught), whereas competition works on the supply side by lowering the expected benefit of donation (the size of the rent times the probability of the rent actually being delivered). If a country is currently in Type III, where most countries are located before making progress, its goal is to reach Type II with the least amount of illegal contributions.

One route to the Type II outcome is an effective system of campaign finance regulation. Although there is no single prescription for success because campaign finance rules have to operate in an environment of institutions and legal culture that varies across countries, experience shows that a well-designed system of regulations should be based on a selection of the following mechanisms: disclosure rules, spending/contribution limits, and public subsidies (Mann 2001, Ewing 2001). Depending on which one of these three mechanisms is most salient, a country can be said to pursue a paradigm based on transparency, regulations, or public funding. (Ackerman and Ayres 2002)

The important part of a campaign finance system is a set of rules on implementation, that is, the assignment of regulatory authority and penalties. To deter violators, regulators must have adequate authority to investigate and sanction. The level of compliance is also affected by the completeness and enforceability of regulations themselves. When regulations are incomplete (permitting a large number of loopholes) and unrealistically restrictive, compliance is expected to be weak. Compatibility with local conditions is another factor in the success of enforcement. Some regulations may fail because they require kinds of administrative capacity, income or supporting institutions that do not exist.

Enforcement, however, does not exist in a political vacuum. Even

---

strengthen regulation and political competition, while the last two, to enhance economic competition.

if good rules that can be enforced are provided for, they will not be enforced without the actions of law enforcement officials. The key question becomes how to make electoral authorities, prosecutors, and judges perform their duties. One important condition is that law enforcement officials have to be held accountable. Experience also shows that political independence is a key condition for their reliability.

The second route is indirect, involving changes in the political and economic environment. As Figure 1 shows, the type of political exchange and the amount of illegal contributions can change if the ruling party becomes less dominant in electoral competition and the economy becomes more competitive. Thus, the key driver of change on the second route is competition, both political and economic. As is true for other types of corruption, the role of competitive pressures can be an important aspect of a strategy to deter illegal campaign contributions (Rose-Ackerman 1978).

Regulation and competition are not mutually exclusive. In the long run, both regulation and competition are needed in order to ensure a reasonable degree of transparency in campaign finance and rein in the costs of elections. Conceptualization of regulation and competition as two alternative paths to reform, however, raises a couple of interesting empirical issues. First, it begs the question of which alternative is more effective under which conditions. Answers to this question can lead to a design of an effective reform strategy. The second issue is more positive, namely, which alternative tends to be adopted first and what are the exact mechanisms through which competition leads to the weakening of the ruling party.

## Evolving Patterns in Presidential Campaign Finance

An image of "grand corruption" was firmly engraved in the folklore of Korean money politics when the details about the fund-raising schemes of two former presidents, Chun Doo Hwan and Roh Tae Woo, began to surface in 1995. It was revealed that Presidents Chun and Roh amassed 693 billion and 450 billion won, respectively, in illegal contributions during their terms; President Chun served from 1981 to 1988, succeeded by President Roh from 1988 to 1993. What was more shocking, even to seasoned observers of Korean politics, was that they took staggering amounts of leftover funds with them when they left office: Chun and Roh admitted to having taken home W160 billion and W230 billion, respectively. Although people had long known that the president's office was the central clearing house of political contributions during the Chun and Roh administrations and did suspect that the former presidents retained some of the funds for their postretirement political activities, no one thought in their wildest dreams that they would keep a combined total of nearly W400 billion for personal use.

Given that these two former presidents were political partners who successfully engineered the victory of their party (Democratic Justice Party) in the 1987 presidential election, a rare event in the history of democratization when the ruling party of the authoritarian regime had won the first election held under democracy, one can imagine the magnitude of money spent on the 1987 presidential election by the Democratic Justice Party. Indeed, the 1995–96 investigations of the former presidents' secret funds provided a rare glimpse into the inner world of presidential campaign finance.

*The 1987 Pattern.* Let's first look at how money was raised for the 1987 presidential campaign. Both the incumbent president (Chun Doo Hwan) and the presidential candidate (Roh Tae Woo) accepted large amounts of illegal contributions from major corporations. Since Roh was not investigated in 1995–6 for his role in the Democratic Justice Party's financing of the 1987 presidential campaign, not much is known about the amounts of money he himself raised. We have a much better idea about when and how Chun raised money—and how much.

During the 1996 investigation of Chun's secret funds, Chun confessed to the prosecutors that he received W696 billion in political contributions during his seven-year rule. The sheer amount of the funds that he had at his disposal gives credence to the rumor that he contributed W150 billion to Roh's 1987 campaign out of the W200 billion Roh raised for that purpose. Given the importance of the 1987 election, it is very plausible that Chun made this kind of all-out effort to raise money.

But actual amounts are not known because the prosecutors could confirm only the transactions involving W216 billion out of a total of W696 billion that Chun admitted to having received in unofficial contributions. They could not press charges against him for the rest, amounting to W480 billion, because they were not able to secure enough evidence (and it is also possible that they considered them as customary, though illegal, political contributions).

Nevertheless, the portions made public confirm that fund-raising activities intensified during the campaign period. Let's look at the monthly count of the payments to Chun from 1982 to 1987 (Table 2) based on the written arraignment. It shows that 38.3 percent of the confirmed transactions were made in the four months leading up to the December 1987 presidential election; the fund-raising campaign typically begins in September. Thus, we can take the funds raised during this four-month period to be campaign funds. Now if the same ratio (38.3 percent) of confirmed campaign funds to total amount of confirmed contributions held for all funds, including the unconfirmed, we can estimate Chun's total campaign funds to be W263 billion, 38.3 percent of the total amount of W696 billion. It is about W63 billion more than the widely quoted figure of W200 billion. Therefore, we can accept the estimate of W200 billion with a reasonable level of confidence. Since their relationship cooled somewhat during the campaign, it is also plausible that Chun did not give all the campaign funds to Roh. So the actual amount of money that Chun contributed to the campaign may have been close to W150 billion, as has been reported in the media.

The 1995–96 investigations also revealed how money was raised

Table 2. The Monthly Count of Illegal Payments to Chun Doo Hwan from 1982 to 1987 (in billion won)

| Month/Year | 1982 | 1983 | 1984 | 1985 | 1986 | 1987 |
|---|---|---|---|---|---|---|
| January | | | 0 | 2.0 | | 1.0 |
| February | | | 0 | | | |
| March | | | | | | 5.0 |
| April | | | | | | |
| May | | | | 1.0 | 3.0 | 0.5 |
| June | | | 5.0 | 1.5 | | 7.0 |
| July | | 7.0 | | 5.0 | | 2.0 |
| August | | | | | 15.0 | 3.0 |
| September | | | | 4.0 | | 17.0* |
| October | | 3.0 | 2.0 | | | 42.3* |
| November | | 0* | 4.0 | 1.0 | | 11.8* |
| December | 3.0 | 4.0* | 15.0 | 14.0 | 20.5 | 11.1* |
| (Yearly total) | (3.0) | (14.0) | (26.0) | (28.5) | (38.5) | (101.0) |

Two payments of 1.0 billion in November 1980 and 2.0 billion in the spring of 1981 were excluded.
*Campaign seasons (February 1984 National Assembly and December 1987 presidential elections)

for the presidential campaign. According to the indictment, Chun's fund-raising method was direct and top-down. The leader of each of the top business groups was expected to give up to W5 billion directly to the president every time they met in the president's private office. The investigations also partly confirmed the stories that Chun received such political contributions on three types of occasions. The first type was regular payments ahead of two main holidays, Thanksgiving and New Year's Day. Data show that the end-of-the-year holiday brought in more money than the Korean Thanksgiving Day, which usually falls in September or October. In fact, Thanksgiving payments began only in 1985. Business leaders also paid the president when they wanted to win favors from him, usually government contracts and tax benefits. The last type of occasion was national elections. Since 1982, when Chun began to receive political contributions from business leaders, two national elections had been held, the February 1984 National Assembly election and the December

1987 presidential election. But data show that Chun was not personally active in financing the February 1984 National Assembly election.

In 1987, Chun Doo Hwan was not alone in soliciting illegal donations from business leaders. According to most accounts, the ruling
party's candidate, Roh Tae Woo, began to accept illegal contributions
close to the election in November. Many companies reportedly gave
both to the incumbent president and the candidate at the same time.
Unfortunately, much less is known about the direct contributions to
Roh because the 1995–96 probes into his finances focused on the
money he raised as president. President Kim Young Sam, who pros-
ecuted the two former presidents at the time, was reluctant to and
did not investigate the funding of the presidential election of 1987
because he himself had been a candidate in that election and was
not free of law violations himself. He was even more reluctant to
investigate the 1992 election, in which he ran as the ruling party
candidate. Thus, it may not be a coincidence that the prosecutors in
1996 did not link any funds that Roh raised in the 1992 campaign
period (September–December) to campaign fund-raising, a finding
not consistent with common expectations (see Table 3).

Because Kim Young Sam did not investigate Roh Tae Woo's campaign finances, we can only guess how much money Roh was able to
raise in the 1987 election. Since the most reliable estimate of Chun's
money is W200 billion, Roh is likely to have raised about half that
amount, W100 billion, on his own because when the donors began
to contribute to him in November, they probably split equally between him and Chun. Thus, Chun's and Roh's funds together
amounted to W300 billion, which was available to the ruling party in
the 1987 election.

As to how much of the war chest was actually spent is a different
matter. Since the 1987 election was competitive and the stakes were
high for both the ruling and the opposition parties, most of the funds
raised, especially the money that Roh raised, likely were spent. But

Table 3. The Monthly Count of Illegal Payments to Roh Tae Woo from 1988 to 1993 (in billion won)

| Month/Year | 1988 | 1989 | 1990 | 1991 | 1992 | 1993 |
|---|---|---|---|---|---|---|
| January | 0.0* | | 1.0* | 0.5 | 4.0 | 1.0 |
| February | 0.0* | | 2.0* | 5.0 | 3.0 | |
| March | 9.0* | 5.0 | 3.0* | | 13.0 | |
| April | 0.0* | | 0.0* | 1.0 | | |
| May | 1.0 | | 1.0 | 12.0 | | |
| June | | 0.5 | | | 3.0 | |
| July | | | | 5.9 | | |
| August | 2.0 | | 2.0 | 15.0 | 3.0 | |
| September | 4.0 | 10.0 | 11.0 | 23.0 | 14.0* | |
| October | | | 1.0 | 1.0 | 2.0* | |
| November | | | 10.0 | 6.0 | 0.0* | |
| December | 17.0 | 19.0 | 31.0 | 25.0 | 5.0* | |
| (Yearly total) | (33.0) | (34.5) | (63.0) | (87.4) | (43.0) | (1.0) |

Two payments of 1.0 billion in November 1980 and 2.0 billion in the spring of 1981 were excluded.
*Campaign seasons (February 1984 National Assembly and December 1987 Presidential elections)

certainly, the campaign did not exhaust Chun's secret funds. He allegedly gave only 75 percent of the campaign funds he raised to Roh Tae Woo and the party. In the end, he was able to walk out of his office with W160 billion even after giving W60 billion of the leftover funds to Roh after the election.

Information on the finances of the opposition candidates is scarce because they have not been investigated since. One reason for this gap is that the two leading opposition candidates of the 1987 election, Kim Young Sam and Kim Dae Jung, have won the presidency in succession and been able to block official investigations. Kim Young Sam had two chances in 1992 and 1997 to investigate Kim Dae Jung's secret funds, but decided not to pursue. While president, Kim Dae Jung, in turn, never attempted to open Kim Young Sam's books. It seems that both men, who had together risen on the opposition side under the authoritarian rule, had a tacit agreement to cooperate.

Although there is no basis to make educated guesses, both Kim

Young Sam and Kim Dae Jung likely raised and spent substantial amounts of money in the 1987 election because they had reasonable chances in that year. When an election is competitive, large donors tend to hedge. In 1987, they reportedly gave generously to all candidates even though they contributed most to their favored candidate, Roh Tae Woo.

Thus, the picture emerging out of the 1987 election is grim. First, both the incumbent president and the ruling party candidate solicited and received unprecedented amounts of illegal donations in the range of W300 billion. Second, the opposition candidates were also able to raise substantial amounts because their probability of winning was not small. Thus, the opposition candidates, especially the more moderate Kim Young Sam, must have been reasonably competitive in fund-raising against the ruling party candidate, if not the incumbent president. Third, all candidates likely spent almost all the money they raised because the election was close throughout. In a way, the 1987 election was the mother of all corrupt elections in democratic Korea, setting the standard by which the following elections were to be evaluated.

*The 1992 Pattern.* All initial signs pointed to the worsening of money politics in the 1992 election. Like his predecessor, the incumbent president, Roh Tae Woo, had been accumulating large amounts of secret funds. And the ruling party of 1992 was as eager as the ruling party of 1987 to raise money because Chung Joo Young, the founder of the Hyundai Group, decided to enter the race with a decidedly money-oriented campaign strategy. Moreover, the disparity between the ruling and opposition parties in campaign contributions was expected to widen in 1992. Unlike Roh Tae Woo in 1987, Kim Young Sam, now the ruling party candidate, was heavily favored to win in 1992, attracting large sums of contributions to his campaign.

It turned out, however, that the 1992 election differed from the 1987 election in three important ways. First, the role of the incumbent president in campaign finance significantly diminished. According to the official report based on the 1995–96 investigations, Roh Tae Woo allegedly raised W450 billion in the five years (1988–93) he was in office. Of that amount, the prosecutors were able to find evidence for transactions involving W284 billion.

The monthly distribution of transactions to Roh shows that he managed his secret funds differently from Chun. During the Roh administration, Thanksgiving contributions in the month of September became routine. The president seems to have been more active than before in raising money for the National Assembly elections in April 1988 and April 1992. The most significant difference is that Roh raised only W21 billion in the crucial last four months of the 1992 campaign, representing about 5 percent of his total, far lower than the 38 percent under Chun. Moreover, it appears that Roh did not tap much into the existing funds to support Kim Young Sam's campaign. Some advisors to Roh have claimed that he donated W100–150 billion to the party campaign funds even though he did not give directly to Kim Young Sam, a fact that Kim Young Sam has denied. Even if Roh did give money, the controversies surrounding it show that he was not an active participant in the campaign financing game of 1992.

The fact that the incumbent president was not active is also significant because it shows that the balance of power between the contributor and the recipient changed in 1992 in favor of the former. In 1987, firms were forced to respond to the pressure from the incumbent president, who still wielded a considerable amount of power; at that time, no one was sure if Chun Doo Hwan was going to keep his promise to retire peacefully after the election. In 1992, companies responded mainly to the electoral prospects of individual candidates. Therefore, one can say that campaign contributions were supply-driven in 1992 and demand-driven in 1987, moving from Type III (predation) toward Type IV (capture), as shown in Figure 1.

The moderating effect of the incumbent president's diminished role, however, may have been partly offset by a (relative) lack of competition at the polls. Unlike Roh Tae Woo, Kim Young Sam was expected to win easily. The promise of the Kim Young Sam candidacy, which was the second distinguishing feature of the 1992 election, affected the pattern of campaign contributions and spending in several ways. First, Kim Young Sam, without the help of the incumbent president, was able to raise large sums of money directly from business leaders. Second, the ruling party's advantage over the opposition parties in fund-raising was larger in 1992 than in 1987. Third, Kim Young Sam did not have to spend all the funds he raised.

We do not know precisely how much of the campaign funds remained unspent after the election. But several subsequent scandals indicate that it may have been more than W100 billion. First, Kim Young Sam's own son was convicted in 1997 of illegally managing about W12 billion of the leftover campaign funds. Second, the Kim Dae Jung government uncovered in 1999 that W100 billion of government funds (belonging to the Agency for National Security Planning) was illegally diverged to the then-ruling New Korea Party during the 1996 general election campaign. Although the government argued that the funds in dispute were from the general budget accounts, it has been widely suspected that the New Korea Party deposited the leftover funds from the 1992 campaign into the bank accounts used by the agency to avoid possible future scrutiny; it is customary for prosecutors to exclude the agency accounts from investigations because the funds therein are supposed to be used for intelligence activities. Third, Kim Young Sam himself commented more than once that he had so much left from his campaign that his party did not have to resort to illegal contributions from large firms during his term. In one interview, he did not deny that the money he raised during the 1992 campaign was in the range of W200–300 billion. If it is true that there was more than W100 billion in leftover funds, the 1992 election may be characterized by large contributions but relatively modest spending by the ruling party.

The third important difference between the 1992 election and the 1987 election was that before the 1992 election, the relationship between the incumbent president and the ruling party candidate became so estranged that the incumbent president not only abstained from fund-raising, but also left office without transferring parts of his secret funds to his successor.

To sum up, the 1992 election was different in that the relationship between the incumbent president and the candidate of the ruling party became seriously strained and the ruling party candidate was heavily favored early on. The effects on the ruling party's ability to raise money were ambiguous. On the one hand, the ruling party could not count on its own sitting president to deliver campaign funds. On the other hand, it was so far ahead in the polls that money started flowing in to its candidate en masse. There were other consequences. For example, the actual level of spending may have been much lower than the amounts of contributions may indicate, leaving large sums of political funds to use after the election.

*The 1997 Pattern.* The 1997 election set a whole new pattern in presidential campaign financing. First, the incumbent president, Kim Young Sam, had rejected the Chun-Roh model of secret funds management. As soon as he came to office in 1993, he stunned business leaders as well as his own aides by announcing that he would not solicit any political contributions from the private sector. All indications are that he did not break his promise during his rule. Second, the divisions within the ruling party were even worse in 1997 than in 1992. In 1997, the ruling party candidate, Lee Hoi Chang, openly broke with Kim Young Sam, accusing him of secretly supporting an opposition candidate, Lee In Je. Third, Lee Hoi Chang ran as a reform candidate. Being a reform candidate meant that he could not actively seek illegal contributions as his predecessors had done. Fourth, the election returned to being very competitive. In fact, the ruling party candidate trailed the leading opposition candidate, Kim Dae Jung, throughout the campaign.

It appears that the incumbent president, Kim Young Sam, was

out of the money chase altogether throughout the campaign. No story has since surfaced linking Kim Young Sam to any fund-raising transaction on behalf of the candidate of his own party. Whether or not he directed some of his leftover funds, which he did not manage himself, to any campaign is not clear. Given his misgivings about Lee Hoi Chang, he is unlikely to have helped the latter financially. During the campaign, the Lee Hoi Chang camp claimed that Kim Young Sam was behind the candidacy of Lee In Je who left the ruling New Korea Party after losing to Lee Hoi Chang in the race for party nomination. If this was true, Kim Young Sam may have contributed financially to the Lee In Je campaign, but certainly not to the Lee Hoi Chang campaign.

The amount of money flowing into the ruling party candidate significantly fell in 1997. Not only did Lee Hoi Chang refuse to solicit money himself because of his political style, but also he would have had limited success even if he had tried because of his lack of popularity. Because the campaign was experiencing severe fund shortages, three advisors to Lee Hoi Chang decided to solicit contributions themselves. The details about their activities came to light in a postelection investigation by the Kim Dae Jung government. According to the government, the three advisors, acting as intermediaries, received a total of W16.6 billion from corporate donors, mostly in November and December of 1997. This revelation was known as the "Tax-Wind" scandal because many of these funds were arranged through top officials at the National Tax Service. With this investigation, the Kim Dae Jung government wanted to show that Lee Hoi Chang relied on the coercive power of the National Tax Service to extort illegal donations from the private sector. Because the main intermediary, a number two official at the National Tax Service, fled abroad during the investigation, however, the government could not establish that the fund-raising activities of the three advisors were coordinated with their candidate. Regardless of whether Lee Hoi Chang was directly involved, what is remarkable about the scandal is how little, by Korean standards, Lee Hoi-Chang as the ruling party candidate was able to generate.

The 1997 election may have been the first election in which an opposition candidate had a financial edge over the ruling party candidate. After aligning with Kim Jong Pil, the leader of a party based in the central provinces, Kim Dae Jung was finally able to expand support beyond his regional base in the southwest (Cholla provinces). He took a lead in the polls in the early months of the campaign and never looked back. Because Kim Dae Jung was the leading candidate throughout the campaign, donors would have been much more willing to contribute to his campaign in 1997 than before. Besides, Kim Dae Jung had already had sizable secret funds even before the campaign. Secret investigations into the Kim Dae Jung funds by the Kim Young Sam government, which did not lead to formal indictments, reportedly found that they were close to W100 billion. Thus, in all likelihood, the incumbency advantage in campaign fund-raising all but disappeared in 1997.

The level of illegal contributions likely fell in 1997. Contributions to the ruling party, which usually account for the vast majority of money raised, drastically fell, and it is unlikely that Kim Dae Jung as an opposition candidate was able to raise enough money to match previous levels of incumbent fund-raising even though he had much more success this time. Since Lee Hoi Chang was able to narrow the margin toward the end of the campaign, it is inconceivable that both camps had a lot of unspent funds at the end of the campaign. Thus, one can say that a medium level of contributions and spending characterized the 1997 election.

*The 2002 Pattern.* Conditions for the December 2002 election were again favorable for a relatively clean election. The "tyranny" of the single-term presidency raged. The ruling party, the Millennium Democratic Party, was so divided over its candidate, Roh Moo Hyun, that many of its legislators left the party in the middle of the campaign. Because of this internal conflict, Kim Dae Jung as the incumbent president did not actively intervene on Roh's behalf. Neither did Roh seek Kim Dae Jung's support. The scandal-ridden Kim Dae Jung administration became a liability for Roh, who wanted to project a reformist image.

The election was also competitive. Throughout the campaign, no candidate was comfortably ahead. Although Lee Hoi Chang was the leading candidate until Chung Mong Joon, a third-party candidate, dropped out of the race,[5] his approval ratings never went above 38 percent. After Chung left the race, Roh did become the front-runner, but his lead over Lee was not considered safe, as the actual election margin of victory, 2.3 percent, attested. In 2002, the ruling party was too weak to emulate the Chun-Roh model of campaign finance even had it wanted to do so.

In fact, no candidate in 2002 desired to adopt the old model of campaign finance. Every candidate had to be a reform candidate because of the importance of young voters, who made up more than 50 percent of the voting population. Because of stronger corporate governance and financial regulations, companies could not easily make unofficial donations. LG Gas, for example, publicly disclosed that it had donated W2 billion to the Grand National Party in September 2002.

Due to these structural factors, the 2002 presidential election was projected to be the cleanest election ever. In terms of the inter-party distribution of money, the ruling party did not have an advantage; Lee Hoi Chang as an opposition candidate was expected to raise more money than the other candidates, including the ruling party candidate.

In 2003–04, an eight-month-long investigation of the financing of the 2002 campaigns confirmed these optimistic expectations. Ac-

5. In an attempt to field a candidate that could defeat Lee Hoi Chang, Roh Moo Hyun and Chung Mong Joon agreed to unify their tickets on the basis of a two- candidate public poll and Roh Moo Hyun was declared the winner on November 24, 2004, a month before the Election Day.

cording to the prosecutors, the Roh Moo Hyun campaign raised W11.9 billion in illegal funds, much less than the W82.3 billion raised by the Lee Hoi Chang campaign. Although these sums were not small by any measure, the fact remains that illegal corporate contributions to the ruling party were at a surprisingly low level. The level of corruption in the opposition Grand National Party should also be put into perspective. Given the length and intensity of the investigations against the Grand National Party, it is fair to say that what was discovered in the end is close to the actual amount of illegal contributions, suggesting that the "grand corruption" pattern of the 1987 and 1992 elections was absent in 2002.

*Evolving Patterns.* Since 1987, a few patterns have emerged that may endure in the future (Table 4). In terms of process, the role of the incumbent president has clearly diminished. Over time, the incumbent president became unwilling to manage large secret funds, raise money for his successor, or channel existing funds, if such existed, to his party. Neither do candidates want to get involved with the types of predatory fund-raising activities that we saw in 1987 and 1992. The second trend is that elections continue to be competitive, resulting in the relatively even distribution of campaign funds.

A combination of these two trends has had predictable effects on the overall level of contributions and spending and the inter-party parity in campaign spending. The amounts of money raised by the ruling party have decreased over time. Since the opposition parties have a limited ability to mobilize funds on a grand scale, a significant decrease in ruling party spending implies that the overall level of spending is also on a downward trend. With a divided ruling party, the opposition parties have been able to raise large contributions themselves, narrowing the gap in campaign funds with the ruling party. In terms of my typology, the type of political exchange began at Type III in 1987 and moved toward Type II in the subsequent elections.

Table 4. Evolving Patterns of Presidential Campaign Finance: The Case of the Ruling Party

| | 1987 | 1992 | 1997 | 2002 |
|---|---|---|---|---|
| Strength of the ruling party | Coherent | Divided | Fractured | Fractured |
| (vote share/margin of victory (%) | Competitive (35.9 / 8.4) | Competitive (41.4 / 8.0) | Less competitive (38.2 / −1.4) | Less competitive (48.9 / 2.3) |
| Market orientation of the economy | Weak | Weak | Medium | Strong |
| Role of the Incumbent President | | | | |
| Maintained secret funds? | Yes | Yes | No | Yes |
| Solicited political contributions? | Yes | Yes | No | No |
| Raised money for the ruling party candidate? | Yes | Limited | No | No |
| Contributed to the campaign? | Yes | Yes | No | Unlikely |
| Ruling Party Candidate | | | | |
| Accepted illegal donations? | Yes | Yes | Limited | Limited |
| Illegal contributions to the ruling party | Very high (W 300 billion)* | High (W200 billion)* | Low (W16.6 billion) | Low (W11.2 billion) |

*Estimated

Figure 2. The Korean System of Presidential Campaign Finance

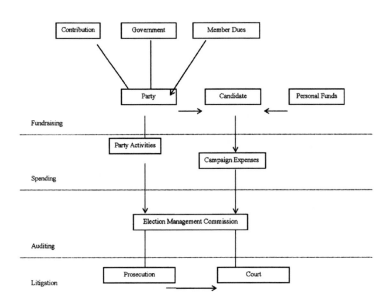

## Key Drivers of Change

How do we account for the evolving patterns of presidential campaign finance? The first place to examine is the formal system of campaign finance that regulates the types and amounts of contributions and expenditures with certain disclosure requirements. Equally important is the effectiveness with which the campaign finance laws are enforced. Economic competition may provide another answer, so I examine the possible effects of economic liberalization on the transparency and level of campaign finance. Political competition offers the final direction of inquiry. The key question with regard to party competition is the electoral competitiveness of the ruling party.

*Better Regulations?* The basic characteristics of Korea's presidential campaign finance system are that it is candidate-centered and expenditure-control–centered. It is the candidate, not the party, who is responsible for complying with complex and strict regulations, especially the level and types of spending allowed. Official spending limits for major party candidates reached about W30 billion in the 2002 election. On the income side, the main restrictions are placed on the sources of income. Presidential candidates can rely only on party grants and personal funds because they are not allowed to raise funds directly from individuals and companies.

Restrictions on party activities are less stringent. For example, parties are not subject to spending limits even though what counts as a party activity is officially stipulated. Since party funds are the only realistic legal source of income for candidates unless they are personally wealthy, it is important to understand how parties raise money to support their candidates as well as their own party activities during the campaign.

During the period under study, restrictions on party activities were less strict. For example, parties were not subject to spending limits even though what counts as a party activity was officially stipulated. Since party funds were the only realistic legal source of income for candidates unless they were personally wealthy, it is important to understand how parties raised money to support their candidates as well as their own party activities during the campaign.

There are three legal sources of income for political parties, private contributions, public subsidies and membership dues. Before 2004, a party was allowed to form one fund-raising committee that could raise up to W60 billion in an election year (W30 billion in a non-election year) but could spend only two-thirds of the revenue. Donors, individuals or companies, could gave money to the fund-raising committee, subject to varying annual and per-case limits on contributions. In 2004, however, the National Assembly voted to ban fund-raising by political parties as well as political contributions by corporations.

Government subsidies have been an increasingly important source of income for political parties. There are two kinds of subsidies, administrative and election. As of 2004, both annual administrative subsidies and election subsidies for each national election amounted to about W10 billion for major parties. Membership dues are collected mostly from party leaders with important party positions, not from rank-and-file members. Before 2004, major sources of income were different for ruling and opposition parties; for opposition parties, government subsidies were most important while private contributions were the largest source for ruling parties. Membership dues accounted for about 10 percent and tended to be least important.

Compared with the restrictiveness of spending/contribution limits, disclosure requirements are week in Korea. Both candidates and parties are required to submit financial statements to the electoral authorities (Election Management Commissions) after the election. But accounting standards are weak. Before 2004, the names of contributors were neither released to the public nor reported even to regulators.

A poor compliance record makes it difficult to argue that campaign finance rules (or better ones) have helped reduce the level of illegal corporate donations since 1987. As we have seen, former presidents and ruling party candidates have broken the law on at least three different accounts. First, it was illegal for anyone other than the party committee to receive private contributions during the presidential election. Second, the sizes of contributions from corporate donors were well over formal contribution limits. Third, they raised and spent money well over the contribution and spending limits.

Some say that the regulations themselves are problematic. First, spending and contribution limits are unrealistically low; they must be adjusted to reflect the reality of high-cost campaigns in Korea. Second, candidates are not allowed to raise money for their campaigns. Although the party fund-raising committee can be used indirectly, it is not a perfect substitute. When a National Assembly election and a presidential election are held in the same year, as in 1992, the party's fund-raising can exceed the annual limits even before the presidential election if the National Assembly election happens to be expensive. The candidate's ability to control party funds is also questionable. Even if party funds are available, candidates may not spend them the way they prefer because party leaders, not candidates, officially control the funds.

There is, however, some evidence that the quality of regulations has improved to induce more compliance. The expansion of public subsidies since 1987, in particular, may have been most important in this regard. Since 1987, the contributions of each voter to subsidy funds have doubled from W400 to W800. More important, election subsidies have been added since 1992. The government now gives political parties an equivalent of their annual administrative subsidies (about W10 billion) as campaign funds for every national election. Thus, in 2002, presidential candidates of major parties started their campaigns with at least W10 billion in public funds. Even though public funding may be much less than the total level of spending, it is still substantial enough to start a competitive campaign. In addition, it should be noted that other legal channels of campaign financing have been expanded; for example, the ceilings on party fundraising had increased to W60 billion by 1997. Therefore, candidates' incentives to seek illegal funds have been substantially reduced.

*Stronger Enforcement?* The issue of enforcement is also controversial. On the one hand, there is strong evidence that enforcement (in the sense of voluntary efforts by law enforcement officials) has been failing. The National Election Management Committee and the Offices of Public Prosecutors, who are responsible for enforcing the regulations, have had little success deterring illegal contributions and expenditures during presidential campaigns. Neither have there been thorough postelection examinations of the funding activities of all major candidates.[6]

6. The post-2002-election investigations may not have been an exception. There is a limit to what the prosecutors can do to investigate the incumbent president. They themselves admitted to this problem when they complained about the reluc-

One problem hampering long-term investigations is that the statute of limitations on violations of campaign laws is only six months. Another reason for lax enforcement is the fear of constitutional breakdown. Since so much is riding on the smooth transition of power, the electoral authorities and the prosecutors are afraid to investigate major party candidates during (because it will disrupt the election and possibly render it illegitimate) and after the election (because it has to investigate a sitting president in the case of the winner and it invites charges of political persecution in the case of the losers). Critics' evaluations are harsher; they complain that regulators and prosecutors do not properly conduct investigations because of their ties to political leaders.

On the other hand, periodic investigations of presidential candidates and the political funds of preceding governments have taken place since 1987 (see Table 5). President Kim Young Sam in 1995–96 investigated the secret political funds of the previous two governments even though he consciously sidestepped the issue of campaign funds. Kim Young Sam was not as tactful toward Chung Joo Young; immediately after the 1992 election, he indicted Chung of illegally channeling W50.9 billion of corporate funds into his campaign. Kim Dae Jung also investigated the campaign funds of his main electoral rival, Lee Hoi Chang. Although most of these investigations were politically motivated, rather than motivated by a desire to clean the system, they must have raised the costs of collecting illegal funds. Kim Dae Jung's investigation of Lee Hoi Chang's funds, in particular, was a reminder to future candidates that their campaign funds are not exempt from scrutiny if they lose.

*Greater Economic Competition?* At the same time, continuing economic reforms since the economic crisis of 1997 have made it difficult for companies to make illegal donations to politicians and for

tance of corporate donors to answer questions regarding possible contributions to the Roh Moo Hyun camp.

Table 5. Postelection Political Scandals

| | | Political Scandals/Investigations | | |
| Presidential Election Year | Targets | Type of Funds (Amount uncovered) | Outcomes |
| --- | --- | --- | --- |
| 1987 | Chun Doo Hwan | Political funds (W18.9 billion) | Apology and exile |
| 1995/1996 | Roh Tae Woo Chun Doo Hwan | Political funds (W450 billion) (W696 billion) | Indicted |
| 1992 | Chung Joo Young | Campaign funds (W50.9 billion) | Indicted |
| 1994/1997 | Kim Dae Jung | Political funds | Not charged |
| 1997 | Kim Hyun Chul | Leftover campaign funds (W12 billion) | Indicted |
| 1999 | Grand National Party | Leftover campaign funds (W100 billion) | Indicted |
| 1998 | Lee Hoi Chang | Campaign funds (W16.6 billion) | Indicted |
| 2003/2004 | Lee Hoi Chang Roh Moo Hyun | Campaign funds (W82.3 billion) (W11.9 billion) | Indicted |

politicians to hide their funds. The most important driver of corporate reform has been foreign investment. Foreign investors now own more than 40 percent of market capitalization and majority shares of most blue-chip companies, who used to make large contributions. Increasing foreign ownership, together with much stronger regulations and active minority shareholders, has significantly improved the transparency and accountability of corporate managers.

Financial transparency has also improved. Gradually, the government has been losing control over commercial banks. Foreign investors have also demanded more disclosure and accountability from those firms and banks in which they are investing. As a result, unless politicians are willing to engage in sophisticated forms of money laundering, it is very difficult to hide large sums of money in the official banking system.

The reduced role of government in the economy can also reduce the supply of political contributions because the benefits of contributions are likely to decrease for donors. Under the new environment, politicians will have more difficulty delivering benefits such as tax breaks and government contracts to their contributors. However, the benefits of structural economic reforms will accrue gradually. Since they are relatively recent phenomena, their lasting effects will not be apparent for the time being, and they are of limited value in explaining the past.

The final hypothesis links increased political competition to the weakening of the ruling party and the resulting reduction in illegal donations. Since democratization began in 1987, some increase in political competition was expected. But the actual change was much more drastic because of the interaction of democracy with two unforeseen phenomena, the rise of reform voters, induced by generational change, and the dynamics of a single-term presidential system.

*Rising Influence of Reform Voters.* Since the early 1990s, a bloc of reform-oriented voters has been gaining influence in electoral politics; reform voters have become critical swing voters because two

opposing regional groupings have been evenly matched in recent elections. Therefore, candidates on both sides of the political spectrum
now realize that they have to avoid corrupt practices to win support
from reform voters. In 1997, Lee Hoi Chang was the one who had
to largely forgo old practices of fund-raising in an effort to appeal to
reform voters. In 2002, every candidate faced similar pressure to be-
have. The influence of the reform voter is likely to grow, as reform-
oriented young voters in their 20s and 30s now comprise more than
50 percent of the electorate.

   *The Dynamics of a Single-Term Presidency.* Two other developments since 1987 have had direct impact on the patterns of presidential campaign finance: the diminished role of the incumbent president in campaign finance and the competitiveness of presidential
elections.

   These two developments are largely a product of none other than
the single-term presidential system. Under the single-term presidential system, the incumbent president and the candidate of the ruling
party have found it almost impossible to cooperate during the campaign. Although both sides have contributed to the deterioration of
their relationship, it has usually been the candidate who wanted to
distance himself from the incumbent president. Although it is difficult to say that it is an inevitable feature of the single-term presidential system, the fact is that every president since 1987 left office either
in disgrace or unpopular. Therefore, every ruling party candidate had
to disassociate himself from the incumbent administration early on
even if he would have to lose the resources that the incumbent president could bring. Incumbent presidents, for their part, were reluctant
to help their candidates because they were more concerned about
their reputation and survival after the election. For them, it was more
important to ensure survival by maintaining neutrality than to ensure
the victory of their untrustworthy successor.

   Another effect of the single-term presidency is that opposition
parties have been able to unite behind a single candidate while ruling

parties have always suffered succession crises. Every winning candidate has tried to control his party after the election in an effort to consolidate power and has not allowed his potential to emerge until the last year of his rule. As a result, opposition candidates usually have had a head start over ruling party candidates, which helped make elections competitive. When divisions within the ruling party worsened beyond repair in 1997, an opposition party was even able to win, the first time in Korean history.

Once the election became competitive and the incumbent president remained largely neutral, the ruling party candidate became incapable of "extorting" large sums of contributions because of his weak leverage without the support of the incumbent president. His problem grew much worse when they were behind in the polls. Thus, the system of campaign finance has naturally evolved from a demand-driven to a supply-driven system, bringing about a more equal distribution of power between donors and the ruling party and a decrease in the amount of money supplied.

## Conclusion

Given the small number of cases (*four* elections since 1987), it is difficult to evaluate the relative importance of different variables in accounting for the observed pattern of presidential campaign finance. In all four areas (regulation, enforcement, economic competition, and political competition), we have seen signs of improvement. The change, however, has been limited in all but one area, the effect of political competition. Increased public funding has reduced the pressure on candidates to seek illegal funds, but campaign finance rules in general remain inadequate, trying to satisfy the political interests of incumbent politicians (e.g., weak regulatory authority) on the one hand and the unrealistic expectations of the public (e.g., strict spending limits and a ban on private contributions to candidates) on the other. Neither is the system of enforcement self-sustaining; regulators and prosecutors seem to act only to meet the political needs of the incumbent president. An improvement in corporate governance and financial market transparency can help stem the flow of illegal funds into political campaigns, but the effects are yet to be realized in full force.

By contrast, the change in party competition has been most drastic. The party system has become competitive even to the point of being fragmented. At the general elections, too, party competition has intensified; no party had won an outright majority before 2004. The fragmentation of the party system weakens the ability of the ruling party to govern. But as I described above, presidential campaign finance is one area in which party competition has had a positive impact.

Despite the noted progress, however, it is unclear whether the Korean system of presidential campaign finance can continue to guard itself from the potential forces of grand corruption. The analysis of the four presidential elections since 1987 suggests that large-scale illegal fund-raising may reappear in future elections if elections become uncompetitive with clear front-runners. Donors looking for political favors will find a way to channel money into campaigns. These donors do not have to be large corporations. Small- and medium-sized companies not only have enough resources to corrupt the system, but also are less subject to public scrutiny because of their size. All major recent scandals have involved such companies.

The problem is, of course, an ineffective system of regulation. Even though some progress has been made in the areas of public funding and enforcement, the overall quality of the regulatory system is too poor to deter those determined to abuse the system, especially during a campaign period. Therefore, efforts to strengthen the regulatory system must continue. In the short run, the role of watchdog organizations such as NGOs and the media will be important. In the medium-to-long run, further institutional reforms are clearly needed. Among the measures being debated now, the independence of the public prosecutors seems to be a top priority on everyone's list. Other measures on the reform agenda are designed to streamline the division of labor among regulatory agencies and to increase the accountability of party leaders in managing party finance.

## References

Ackerman, Bruce and Ian Ayres. *Voting with Dollars: A New Paradigm for Campaign Finance*. New Haven, Conn.: Yale University Press, 2002.

Ansolabehre, Stephen, John de Figueiredo, and James Snyder. "Why Is There So Little Money in U.S. Politics?" Working paper, Department of Political Science, MIT, Cambridge, Mass., 2002.

Chafuen, Alejandro and Eugenio Guzman. "Economic Freedom and Corruption." In *2000 Index of Economic Freedom*, edited by Kim Holms O'Driscoll and Melanie Kirkpatrick, Washington, D.C.: Heritage Foundation, 2000.

Ewing, Keith. "Corruption in Party Financing: The Case for Global Standards." In *Global Corruption Report 2001*. Berlin: Transparency International, 2001.

Kang, David. "Bad Loans to Good Friends: Money Politics and the Developmental State in Korea." *International Organization*, 2002.

Mann, Thomas. "Political Science and Campaign Finance Reform: Knowledge, Politics and Policy." Paper for delivery at the 2002 Annual Convention of the American Political Science Association, August 29–September 1, 2002.

Rose-Ackerman, Susan. *Corruption: A Study in Political Economy*. New York: Academic Press, 1978.

The World Bank. *Anticorruption in Transition: A Contribution to the Policy Debate*. Washington, D.C.: World Bank, 2000.

CHAPTER FIVE

# The Formation of the Rule of Law in Corporate Governance

Joongi Kim

## Introduction

After the financial crisis in 1997, Korea conducted an overhaul of its economic and financial regulatory system. Corporate governance in particular was a central target for legal reforms. Despite considerable progress, the rule of law remains elusive in corporate governance in terms of effectively minimizing agency costs associated with controlling shareholders. This chapter will seeks to explore what has hindered the establishment of rule of law in corporate governance. Rule of law will be assessed ultimately through the effective operation and compliance with the laws associated with corporate governance.

This chapter first describes the corporate governance environment in Korea prior to the financial crisis, including the legal changes that have occurred in the postauthoritarian era leading up to the post-financial crisis. This chapter argues that the postauthoritarian legacy in which the state actively intervened in the economic realm still lingers and that the inability to develop an effective infrastructure based upon hard law can be attributed to past over-reliance on soft laws and controls.

Then the gradual emergence of rule of law in terms of corporate governance is reviewed, including a discussion of how the governance of Korean corporations has been influenced in terms of rule of law. The various regulatory developments are covered in terms of hard law

The author would like to thank Jong-Goo Yi for his helpful comments and Hyejin Kim for her assistance in preparing this chapter.

and soft law as well as market practices that have taken place in the postfinancial crisis period. Various court cases are examined to place this analysis into practical perspective, and case studies are presented to show what needs to be done to improve rule of law in corporate governance. And finally, there is a discussion of how rule of law is developing in the corporate sector and what type of rule of law can be anticipated in the future.

Ultimately, this study seeks to determine the rule of law system that has emerged in terms of corporate governance in Korea. To evolve toward a liberal, market economy, effective rule of law in the form of market-based checks and balances must be established. An efficient and disciplined market-based economy will also help prevent the recurrence of such devastation as financial contagion. This chapter therefore argues that Korea's corporate governance is in the process of establishing such much-needed rule of law.

## Exogenous Rule of Law in Corporate Governance Before the Financial Crisis

This section reviews the exogenous rule of law in corporate governance. The time frame of analysis starts from the 1980s and continues up until the financial crisis. It particularly focuses on the effectiveness of the rule of law framework in controlling the agency problem in corporations. First, the relevant definitions of the rule of law are reviewed. Second, the rule of man that prevailed is explored. Third, the legal framework is reviewed through the function of corporate law and the securities law. Fourth, the soft controls that played a function in the governance of corporations are explored.

### Definition of Rule of Law

Precise definitions of the rule of law remain a challenge, and various versions have been proposed. According to Fuller's famous catalogue of the necessary characteristics for the rule of law, the laws should be "general, public, prospective (or at least not abusively retrospective), understandable, consistent (or at least not self-contradictory), capable of being followed, stable, and enforced."[1] Peerenboom categorizes this definition as "thin rule of law" and believes that "thick rule of law" should also be added as a separate type.[2] Thick rule of law, he argues, includes such factors as political morality, economic arrangements, forms of government, and conceptions of human rights.

What follows is an exploration of rule of law in corporate governance largely based upon Peerenboom's framework. Emphasis is placed upon the effectiveness of these laws and their limitations. The legal framework of corporate governance that seeks to minimize the conflicts of interests between controlling shareholders and noncontrolling shareholders is the focus. The legal regime is reviewed in terms of hard law and soft law, or exogenous and endogenous factors. Exogenous factors are covered first.

## Rule of Man, Authoritarian Rule, and Industrial Policy

Until the financial crisis, corporate governance in Korea largely revolved around rule of man in lieu of rule of law. The strong legacy of authoritarian rule and state-led industrial policy prevailed throughout all sectors of society. The country retained many characteristics reminiscent of a strong social welfare state. Faced with legitimacy questions, authoritarian regimes focused their attention on economic growth and prosperity. Strong, state-led growth dominated economic, financial, and corporate development. Vestiges of industrial policy could be found even late into the 1980s.[3] Rule of man in corporate

1. Lon Fuller, *The Morality of Law*, rev. ed. (New Haven, Conn.: Yale University Press, 1969).

2. Randall Peerenboom, "Let One Hundred Flowers Bloom, One Hundred Schools Contend: Debating Rule of Law in China," 23 *Michigan Journal of International Law* 471, 478–79 (2002).

3. Samsung, LG, and Hyundai, for example, entered the semiconductor industry whereas Kia was granted a monopoly in the truck business, while Hyundai and Daewoo were granted a duopoly in the passenger car business.

governance emanated from this political economy because the country was largely ruled through regimes led by authoritarian personalities until 1987. The authoritarian state served as the primary guardian overseeing controlling-shareholders' and the public's interests.

Under industrial policy, policy makers tightly controlled the chaebol, the large, family-dominated conglomerates, while granting them overwhelming privileges in the economy. Serving as the engines of growth for the country, the chaebol were blessed with a wide range of special benefits, ranging from preferential financing, exclusive market arrangements, and trade protections to protections for corporate control.[4] Chaebol-led market dominance in the form of monopolies and oligopolies were condoned. In 1990, for example, 135 markets were characterized by market dominance and almost 80 percent of these were associated with the chaebol. The state granted tax-breaks, permits, and subsidies as well.

The state in turn employed a vast arsenal of methods to control the affairs of companies, particularly through its oversight of the banking and financial system. Companies relied upon state credit provided through indirect or debt financing as the primary means for acquiring capital. The government also had the authority to approve special facility fund loans and the issuance of equities, bonds, and depository receipts. The debt-to-equity ratio of the top 30 chaebol remained around four to one throughout most of the development period. The reliance upon commercial banks for debt-financing served as a powerful control mechanism for the state. The state utilized commercial banks as a financing channel to implement industrial policy and called upon them to serve as the monitors to curb potential corporate excesses and wrongdoing. Given the state's heavy-handed nature, market forces and the rule of law remained underdeveloped. Neverthe-

---

4. Individual investors for example could not acquire more than a 10 percent stake in a listed company without special approval.

less, the economy was marked by "generally good macroeconomic management."[5]

The rule-of-man climate prevalent at the time was best captured in the Constitutional Court's decision that found the government's 1985 breakup of the Kukje Group unconstitutional.[6] The court held that numerous basic freedoms and rights guaranteed under the constitution were violated. Under the constitution, for example, the government could intervene in the management of defunct companies only if it had explicit statutory authority or if it acted according to an emergency decree. The government's breakup of Kukje, however, violated the constitutional right of businesses to be free from "arbitrary and discriminatory treatment." The court stressed that replacing the dominant shareholder and managers of a private enterprise "without legal basis" served to "destroy the market economy and governance by the rule of law." Measures that disregarded proper procedures, despite their purpose, were deemed an abuse of public authority. The court stated that "democracy is the respect of means and procedures, and the ends alone cannot be the primary purpose." Hence, the government's breakup occurred without statutory authority and violated fundamental due process guaranteed under the rule of law.

Korea's authoritarian regimes that operated under the rule of man were often plagued by cronyism, regionalism, and misguided personal loyalty. Without proper accountability, predation and rent-seeking became serious problems. The excessive concentration of power in the political realm created a similar counterpart in the governance structure of corporations. Just as companies that remained in favor with political leaders survived, a similar dynamic emerged within compa-

5. Graham, Edward M. 2003. *Reforming Korea's Industrial Conglomerates* (Washington, D.C.: Institute for International Economics, 2003), 74.

6. Constitutional Court 1993; Huh, Young. 1994. "*Konggwonnyoke uihan Kukje Group haech'eui wibopsong* (The Illegal Break-up of the Kukje Group through Public Authority)," in *P'allyewolpo* Vol. 280:16; Yoon, Dae Gyu. 1995. "New Developments In Korean Constitutionalism: Changes and Prospects." In *Pacific Rim Law and Policy Journal* Vol. 4:413–414.

nies as well. Employees that held the favor of the controlling shareholder would rise to the higher echelons. Just as the head of the country dominated the country, the controlling shareholders unilaterally dictated corporate policy. The weak state of rule of law relative to the rule of man can trace its origins to the industrial policy that created the chaebol and their corporate governance.

The state's political economy was guided by strong central leadership, and corporations were managed according to concentrated decision making. Controlling shareholders of chaebol dominated entire conglomerates, controlling dozens of subsidiaries and related companies while avoiding legal accountability. Controlling shareholders ruled despite marginal ownership portions that were often less than 3 percent. Companies within a conglomerate were held together through intricate cross-shareholding arrangements between related and sister companies. Controlling shareholders acted with regal authority over the entire conglomerate even though they often were registered as the director of only the major corporation of the conglomerate. In any event, since they maintained control, they opted to minimize their legal responsibility and limit their personal investment risk.

The chaebol decision-making model no doubt boasted advantages, efficient and speedy decision making among them. Yet without adequate supervision or monitoring of management, the system harbored potential dangers. What constrained latent hazards of ineffective corporate governance was the authoritarian state led by its powerful and relatively honest rule of man. This served as a substitute for a rule of law in corporate governance that ironically later unraveled with the transition to representative government.

### Underdeveloped Market and Unprepared Rule of Law

With the establishment of a full-fledged democracy in 1988, the rule of man was replaced with an underdeveloped system of rule of law. The roles of the state and autocrats receded, and corresponding regulatory and market-based disciplines in the forms of legal checks and balances were called upon to fill the void. The failure to establish rule of law at this critical juncture contributed to the disastrous consequences of the financial crisis that struck in 1997.

The mix of a decentralized, weakened state and awkward remnants of governmental control fueled corruption and distorted incentives. Companies sought bank loans not based upon merit but by rent-seeking through government officials, powerful politicians, and bank directors. Bank directors did not act on behalf of shareholders, brokering disastrous nonperforming loans that later crippled their banks. Further weakening the state's control, starting from 1988, interest rates were deregulated and policy loans declined to 18 percent of bank credit by 1995.[7] In an attempt to provide independence for banks, privatization was attempted in the mid-1990s. Ultimately, the banking system failed to restructure, and devastating corporate loan scandals ensued.[8] One of the most egregious cases involved the Hanbo Group and its illegal ties with its main bank, Korea First Bank. The collapse of the Hanbo Group led to the takeover of Korea First Bank by the government and became the textbook example of the importance of corporate governance.

Meanwhile, conglomerates adeptly utilized nonbank financial institutions such as life insurance companies, liability insurance companies, investment trusts, and merchant banks for their financing, thereby freeing them from overreliance upon banks. Chaebol rapidly increased their borrowing from these largely unregulated and unprotected nonbank financial intermediaries. By 1991, the portion of borrowing from nonbank financial institutions reached a precarious 45

---

7. Despite these efforts, financial institutions "largely remained under effective governmental control." Graham 2003:59.

8. Joongi Kim, "Recent Amendments to the Korean Commercial Code and Their Effects on International Competition," *University of Pennsylvania Journal of International Economic Law* 21 (2000): 273, 321.

percent among the top 30 chaebol.[9] When the currency crisis hit, however, the loans proved overwhelming.

Korea's equity market in turn remained underdeveloped. Market-based monitoring functions did not emerge effectively. Self-regulatory functions of the stock exchanges, for example, remained weak. Disastrous examples of market intervention can be found. In 1989, to artificially revitalize the stock market the government forced investment trust companies (ITCs) to borrow money to buy listed equities. Government intervention in the investment decisions of ITCs contravened the interests of the ITCs' own shareholders and disregarded the board of directors as well. Later in May 1991, more than 2 trillion won in public money was used to compensate ITCs for these failed equity investments.[10] The burden of the interest payments from these losses would further haunt the ITCs.

After the period of authoritarian rule, the chaebols' corporate structure became more vulnerable to latent risks. The longer an unchecked concentrated system persisted and the larger companies became, the greater the potential agency costs and decline in efficiency. The consequences of an overprotected management lacking accountability over time outweighed the need for efficient, decisive decision making. With the decline of state control, controlling shareholders dominated corporate affairs without any adequate checks and balances regarding their decisions. Many controlling shareholders gravitated toward empire-building, wealth preservation, and the pursuit of other private benefits of control. They took full advantage of the lack of external and internal controls. Without proper accountability and transparency, the agency problem inherent in corporations worsened.

To prevent further improper subsidization of subsidiaries and overexpansion into new business industries and to decentralize control,

9. Sakong, Il. 1993. *Korea in the World Economy*. Washington: Institute for International Economics.

10. Graham 2003:77.

policy makers sought to lure chaebol groups into dispersing their ownership by listing their shares on the stock exchange. Good intentions aside, a critical mistake was committed; the decrease in ownership was not met with a corresponding increase in corporate governance related supervision by such entities as stakeholders and shareholders. The rule of man was replaced by an unprepared, inadequate rule of law system.

### The Restraints of the Legal Environment

Various aspects of Korea's legal environment served to deter the rule of law in corporate governance. First, natural barriers to legal access existed. Attorneys were not accessible. The number of attorneys has only increased in recent years.[11] At less than 0.02 percent of the total population, the number of lawyers was among the lowest in the developed nations. The lack of attorneys also pushed attorney fees to prohibitive highs. Furthermore, Koreans tend to be nonlitigious by nature, and litigation itself could be time-consuming and invite unwanted public exposure.

Second, Korea's civil law tradition provided a weaker environment for corporate governance.[12] General civil law principles, such as the "loser pays" rule that served as a natural deterrent to legal recourse.[13] Civil law countries also lack discovery procedures further curtailing the general lack of information of potential litigants. Another com-

11. 1981: 1000; 1994: 3000; 2002: 5000; 2004: 7000.

12. Stephen J. Choi, "Law, Finance, and Path Dependence: Developing Strong Securities Markets," *Texas Law Review* 80 (2002): 1657, 1660–63; John C. Coffee, Jr., "Do Norms Matter? A Cross-Country Evaluation," University of Pennsylvania Law Review 149 (2001): 2151, 2157–59; John C. Coffee, Jr., "Privatization and Corporate Governance: The Lessons from Securities Market Failure," *Journal of Corporate Law* 25 (1999): 24–25; Simon Johnson et al., "Tunneling, *American Economic Review* 90 (2002): 22–26; Rafael La Porta et al., "Investor Protection and Corporate Governance," *Journal of Financial Economics* 58 (2000): 3–4.

13. The loser pays rule is commonly known as the British rule. Thomas D. Rowe, Jr., The Legal Theory of Attorney Fee Shifting: A Critical Overview, 1982 Duke L.J. 651, 651 (1982).

plication was that despite Korea's civil law tradition its corporate law structure was adopted from the American system. This created an anomalous situation in which a common law based corporate governance system was grafted upon a civil law system that had developed based upon concentrated ownership structures for companies.

Third, prior to the full-fledged democratization process in 1987, legal autonomy was also suspect.[14] Various examples existed where judges were subject to political intimidation and even forced to leave the bench.[15] Minority opinions themselves were rare events. Judges did not receive lifetime appointments, but instead were appointed to fixed terms. Under the authoritarian regimes of the past, this left them susceptible to outside political pressure. Conflicts of interests in the judicial system also remain a problem. Former judges and prosecutors were still free to represent clients before courts or districts where they previously worked without restrictions.[16] They could bring cases in the chambers of their former colleagues right after their departure. Ex parte communications with judges and defendant attorneys also remained a thorny issue in the Korean bar. Various legal decisions later acknowledged that the previous judicial system was unable to offer due process and proper recourse for many parties.[17]

Fourth, judges and prosecutors remained overworked and undertrained in corporate affairs. With little precedence or formal training in corporate cases, judges and prosecutors lacked experience in civil and criminal liability related to corporate defendants. Securities fraud cases against such abusive practices as market manipulation, insider

---

14. Jaegyu Kim Sedition Trial, Supreme Court decision.

15. Id.

16. Current legislative proposals seek to restrict former judges and prosecutors from representing criminal cases in the courts or districts they last served in for a period of two years. Constitutional Court Decision overturning restrictions on where to open law offices. Special courts system for former judges.

17. Kukje Case. Courts subsequently rendered landmark decisions that held that prior governments exceeded their statutory authority due to lack of due process and the failure of rule of law.

trading, and misrepresentation were rare. Unwritten customary law also existed that corporate defendants deserved particular protection due to their enormous contributions to the economy. Furthermore, given the conservative civil law tradition and heavy case loads, courts were constrained in trying to venture into shaping new areas of the law and adopting newer concepts. The legal system and rule of law at the time therefore faced a multitude of challenges.

### Sociocultural Factors in the Rule of Law

Recent studies suggest that greater weight should be placed upon the importance of sociocultural factors and their influence upon the rule of law.[18] These studies emphasize that such factors as group dynamics, paternalism (*onjeongjui*), cultural traditions, and collectivism influenced the formation of the rule of law. According to deeply ingrained factors such as Confucianism, social harmony, order, and righteousness rather than justice were nurtured as the symbol of an ideal society.[19] Under this framework, rule of law is affected because the social fabric places greater importance upon group harmony, generates a tremendous amount of peer pressure, and chills efforts at change.

Confucian collectivist norms, for example, emphasize five traditional relationships: (1) affection between father and son, (2) righteousness between ruler and minister, (3) attention to separate functions between husband and wife, (4) proper order between old and

---

18. Amir Licht, "Legal Plug-Ins: Cultural Distance, Cross-Listing, And Corporate Governance Reform," *Berkeley Journal of International Law* 22 (2004): 195); Franklin A. Gevurtz, "The European Origins And the Spread of the Corporate Board of Directors," *Stetson Law Review* 33 (2004): 925; Bernard S. Black et al., "Corporate Governance in Korea at the Millennium: Enhancing International Competitiveness," *Iowa Journal of Corporation Law* 26 (2001): 537, 545; see generally, Chaihark Hahm, "Law, Culture, and the Politics of Confucianism," *Columbia Journal of Asian Law* 16 (2003): 253.

19. Licht. Confucianism was governing ideology for more than five hundred years.

young, and (5) faithfulness between friends.[20] Obedience within these special relationships, particularly within the family, was critical. In terms of organization structure, Confucianism emphasized strict hierarchical structures. Authority figures commanded loyalty, and they, in turn, were responsible for family members.

Within the corporate context, a similar paradigm prevailed. The controlling shareholder would command the obedience and loyalty of all employees. All members of the corporation were in fact part of one big family with all authority concentrated in the controlling shareholder. In a multilayered system of corporate hierarchy, instructions from the top would not be questioned. Subsidiaries and affiliates within a conglomerate were all part of the family. The interests of the conglomerate as a whole were placed above the interests of individual companies. Profitable companies had an obligation to help their less fortunate affiliates. Employees that sacrificed themselves for the conglomerate would be compensated and protected.

Some assert that sociocultural values were distorted by authoritarian rulers as a means to justify their rule. Under the same reasoning, a similar distortion was conveniently adopted by controlling shareholders as well. The critical problem with this type of sociocultural approach occurs when the interests of the conglomerate or other members diverged from the personal interests of the controlling shareholder or family. The private benefits of control derived solely for the controlling shareholder cannot be justified as beneficial to the conglomerate or its other interested parties as a whole.

## Endogenous Rule of Law in Corporate Governance

An examination of the endogenous rule of law that governs corporations reveals serious defects. The endogenous rule of law reviewed in this chapter focuses on the legal framework that is specific to cor-

---

20. Pitman B. Potter, "Legal Reform in China: Institutions, Culture, and Selective Adaptation," *Law and Social Inquiry* 29 (Spring 2004): 465.

porations, such as the company law and securities law. It will center on those laws that are directly associated with corporate governance. As a whole, the internal functions of the board, directors, statutory auditor, and shareholders did not operate properly. Externally, auditing, public enforcement, private enforcement, the market for corporate control, and disclosure standards all remained weak. Reputational intermediaries such as accounting firms, credit agencies, and self-regulatory organizations also functioned ineffectively. The lack of effective compliance with fiduciary duty remained a fundamental problem. Without a board of directors unable to fulfill its primary responsibility, rule of law in corporate governance had little chance to function properly. Rule of law in corporate governance was substituted by rule of man, the controlling shareholder.

### Directors and Fiduciary Duty

The bedrock principle of corporate law, fiduciary duty, remained a most frequently disregarded legal standard in Korea.[21] The failure of directors to even understand their fiduciary duty demonstrated the ultimate failure of the rule of law in corporate governance. Directors instead had little incentive to favor the interests of the corporation as a whole over the personal interests of the controlling shareholders. This demanded a thankless bravery that would only incur scorn of the controlling shareholder. Hence, directors did not serve as a check and balance to potential expropriation or empire-building committed on behalf of the controlling shareholders. Before the financial crisis, the standard practice was that board of director meetings were not even officially held and minutes were not even taken.[22] The failure of directors to comply with their fiduciary duties created serious prob-

21. Arts. 382, 382–3; Konsik Kim & Joongi Kim, "Revamping Fiduciary Duties: Does Law Matter in Corporate Governance?" in *Global Markets, Domestic Institutions: Corporate Law and Governance in a New Era of Cross-Border Deals*, ed., Curtis J. Milhaupt (New York: Columbia University Press, 2003).
22. Kim, *supra*, note 9.

lems under the legal system because directors also co-functioned as officers.

The first modern decisions that attempted to shape a business judgment rule only emerged after the financial crisis. One of the central reasons that directors failed to comply with their fiduciary duty was that they were never held accountable on those grounds. According to one assessment, "[s]hareholder suits are the primary mechanism for enforcing the fiduciary duties of corporate managers."[23] Korea, of course, never had any shareholder suits. Hence, shareholders could not and did not seek legal redress to hold directors legally accountable for breaches of fiduciary duty. Fiduciary duties were unenforced and neglected as a result.

Remedies for violations of fiduciary duties have also been limited. They consist only of compensatory damages, invalidation of a conflict-of-interest transaction or, more fundamentally, removal of the director. In the United States, in contrast, breaches are reviewed under equity principles and remedies are flexibly fashioned. U.S. shareholders can, for example, sue for disgorgement of a director's improper gains, which acts as a considerable deterrent to abuse. Under Korean law, however, this type of remedy has been recognized only in limited circumstances.

Boards therefore proved ineffective in preventing reckless borrowing, misappropriation, and accounting fraud. Stunning corporate failures during the financial crisis shattered confidence in Korean corporations and showed how important the role of the directors and their fiduciary duty are.

## Strong Controlling Shareholders

Controlling shareholders dictated all board decisions. They self-selected directors and statutory auditors from among the company's employees. The most important criteria in the selection process be-

---

23. Kraakman et. al. 1994: 1733; contra Fischel and Bradley 1986.

came personal loyalty to the controlling shareholder. The lack of labor mobility further forced directors and auditors to remain captive and dependent. Chairmen thus dominated directors and auditors. Many chaebol chairmen gravitated to business strategies that emphasized diversification, size, and market share over profitability and shareholder value. The interests of the entire chaebol conglomerate were placed above the well-being of individual corporations and their respective shareholders. Furthermore, the chance of being held accountable became remote, and investment risk exposure was minimal.

Controlling shareholders dominated their conglomerates without effective checks or balances or accountability. Management structure became plagued with inefficiencies and problems. The failure of corporate governance contributed to the spectacular failures of conglomerates and the banking sector. The problems were compounded by the weak market discipline. Profitable companies supported weaker companies through transfer pricing and cross-guarantees. In the worst cases, the conglomerate was used to extract private benefits of the controlling shareholder through expropriation, creation of slush funds, and self-dealing. Controlling shareholders could reduce their ownership because they could maintain their control through the cross-ownership structure.

### Statutory Auditors

Statutory auditors similarly failed to perform their role as internal watchdogs that monitored board and management decisions. Originally, auditors played a key role as the internal monitors of accounting and decisionmaking over the company. Statutory auditors became positions typically occupied by senior managers before they retired. In other cases, companies recruited senior government officials or retired regulators to fill this prestigious sinecure. In the end, as with other internal checks and balances, corporate law did not operate as planned. Large companies with assets of more than 2 trillion won must now establish audit committees in place of the statutory auditors. An audit committee consisting of outside directors could be more effective in reducing potential conflicts than the previous statutory auditors.

## Weak Shareholders

Shareholders played a marginal role in corporate affairs. They lacked influence and remained passive actors. Poor laws thwarted noncontrolling shareholders in any type of action to protect themselves. Most of the minimum shareholding requirements for exercising shareholder rights were set at prohibitively high levels that effectively froze out shareholders from participating in corporate affairs.[24] Shareholder rights were not exercised and shareholder litigation did not exist. Institutional investors did not participate in corporate affairs because they could not even exercise the voting rights for shares held on behalf of customer accounts.[25]

Shareholders were not interested in participating in corporate governance. Most shareholders did not even realize that they had rights. The primary focus for shareholders was short-term gain rather than long-term investment. A short-term investment strategy led to little loyalty or interest in the affairs of corporate management. Noncontrolling shareholders lacked the ability and interest to participate in corporate affairs, and did not provide any monitoring pressure. Shareholders' meetings became symbolic events that rubber-stamped board decisions. The lack of protection for the interests of noncontrolling shareholders was considered a major barrier to foreign investment.

24. With listed companies averaging 62.3 billion won (U.S. $52 million) in capital stock in 1997, a five percent holding requirement, for instance, meant that interested stockholders would have to amass over 3.1 billion won (U.S. $2.6 million) in shares to exercise their shareholder rights. The lowered minimum holding requirements still require a substantial number of shares. With the average total market value of Korean listed companies at approximately 228 billion won (U.S. $190 million), one percent of the total shares would require shareholders with 2.28 billion won (U.S. $1.9 million) worth of stock.

25. The shares in such accounts could only be exercised through shadow voting.

Policy makers kept the minimum holding requirements high because they believed management needed protection. They believed that management needed to make swift and decisive judgments and could not be burdened by outside pressures such as from shareholders. Lower minimum holding requirements could also expose companies to abuse by bad faith shareholders. Racketeers could acquire shares and threaten to cause trouble at shareholders' meetings, extorting payoffs in return for their cooperation.[26]

### Public Enforcement

A variety of players are responsible for the implementation of public enforcement in the corporate governance framework. They include self-regulatory organizations, regulators, prosecutors, and eventually the courts. Weak public enforcement has been blamed for the failure of effective rule of law in corporate governance. Without the potential of legal accountability, the rule of law could not function properly. Public enforcement in the corporate sector remained weak. Under the Fuller definition of rule of law, lack of effective enforcement emerged as a most problematic issue. Public enforcement at its worst was often inconsistent, unpredictable, opaque, politically motivated, and predatory. This generated popular distrust toward public enforcement and eventually toward the rule of law.

In Korea, the leading players in charge of public enforcement include the Korea Stock Exchange, the Financial Supervisory Commission, the Financial Supervisory Service, the Fair Trade Commission, the National Tax Office, the prosecutors' office, and the courts. Their responsibility ranged from proper disclosure, accounting audits, related-party transactions, and embezzlement or misappropriation to tax evasion, securities fraud, such as market manipulation, and insider trading.

Weak sanctions persisted as a problem. Sanctions were rarely

---

26. Unlike Japan, the activity of racketeers has been marginal at best.

made public and tended to be done anonymously. Instead of firms being sanctioned, individuals were given warnings. Instead of fines, suspensions, disqualifications, or delisting, private warnings were often issued. This pattern of generous enforcement was particularly pervasive in the regulation of companies.

Courts and prosecutors tended to be peculiarly lenient with corporate defendants of large conglomerates. When issuing their judgments, courts did not demonstrate a firm commitment to penalizing defendants. Even in cases of serious crimes or breaches, courts often cited past contributions to the economic development of the country as a reason for commuting punishment or reducing liability.[27] Appellate courts in particular frequently reduced sentences and stayed execution of sentences on these grounds. Instead of receiving stiffer penalties or greater liability to send a message to the marketplace, the courts were more generous with defendants from the largest companies.[28] Ultimately, in the rare case in which courts held against controlling shareholders or senior managers, the defendants received presidential pardons within a short time.[29] Heads of small- and medium-sized companies did not share similar fates. When prosecutors have sought to hold managers accountable, they have not been con-

27. The Seoul High Court affirmed his three-year sentence, but he was granted a stay of execution of the sentence for four years due to his age and "his enormous contributions to the economic development of the country." The Seoul District Court had sentenced Chung to three years imprisonment for multiple violations, including the expropriation of KW 43.3 billion from Hyundai Heavy Industries that were used for his political campaign.

28. This contrasts significantly with stiff sentences in the United States given to high-profile figures such as Bernie Ebbers of WorldCom (25-year sentence) and Jeffrey Skilling of Enron (24 years).

29. In 1990, when Chung was found guilty for another enormous scandal, he was granted a suspended sentenced based upon his contributions to economic development. He was also arrested in 1995 following the slush fund trials involving President Roh Taewoo. Later, however, Chung Taesoo was not so fortunate. Supreme Court, Judgment of December 26, 1997, 97 Do 2609. In April 1998, 18 months were added to Chung's sentence. Seoul District Court, Judgment of Apr. 20, 1998.

sistent in the application of the law.[30] Until recently, prosecutors placed a lesser emphasis on white-collar crimes.

The Korea Stock Exchange and the Korea Listed Company Association have been inactive in policing their industries. At most, the New Offering Adjustment Committee denied equity issuances or bond offerings for companies that had fallen out of favor were often denied.[31] As for the tax authorities, selective use of tax audits served as a tool against curbing potential insider abuses.[32] More often tax audits were politically motivated affairs.

*Private Enforcement*

As mentioned previously, private enforcement in the form of shareholder legal action remained underutilized. In the case of derivative actions, the prohibitive 5 percent shareholding limit was finally reduced to 1 percent in 1998. The Securities Exchange Act was then repeatedly amended, and shareholders of listed firms holding 0.0001 percent of the shares for six months may now file a derivative suit (Art.191-13(1)). Despite the lowered thresholds, only a few reported shareholder derivative suits have been brought since 1997. Concerns about extortionist litigation have not materialized and many observers have pointed out that the courts can deal with concerns over bad faith litigation.

Shareholders brought the first derivative action in Korea in 1997 against Korea First Bank (KFB) directors.[33] Saddled with more than

30. Kim and Kim, note 22.

31. Hyundai Machine and Hyundai Lumber's applications to issue KW 48.9 billion and KW 19.8 billion in new equity respectively in 1992.

32. In January 1992, for instance, the National Tax Office levied a charge of KW 136.1 billion to the Hyundai Group as a result of its tax audit in the year that its Chairman ran for the presidential election. In August 1992, Chung Mong Hun, Chairman of Hyundai Merchant Marine, was sentenced to 3 years with a 5-year stay of execution and fined KW 12 billion and forced to return KW 13.4 billion for tax evasion and falsification of company documents.

33. Supreme Court 2002.3.15; Suwon District Court 98 Gahap 22553, 2001.12.17

1 trillion won in bad debts from Hanbo and other failed corporates, KFB eventually had to be nationalized and later became the first commercial bank in Korea taken over by foreign interests. In the end, KFB's directors were held liable for accepting bribes and illegally granting bad loans.[34] This resulted in the first civil judgment against directors for breaching their fiduciary duty. Another prominent court decision found that the directors of Samsung Electronics were liable for breaching their fiduciary duty as well.[35] The recent increase in directors' liability insurance has been cited as a negative aspect of shareholder-driven private enforcement. In 1997, only one company had director liability insurance, whereas in 2004, more than 300 companies have adopted such policies. Yet these insurance policies are testimony to the perceived potential legal risk associated with being a director. In the past, the market had simply determined there was no legal risk or accountability. In the end, derivative actions have not provided sufficient redress for injured shareholders.

### Reputational Intermediaries

Reputational intermediaries such as accounting firms, investment banks, credit agencies, and other financial institutions likewise did not provide sufficient discipline. None of these reputational intermediaries curtailed the controlling shareholder. Unlike the corporate governance systems in Japan or continental Europe, financial intermediaries failed to offer sufficient supervisory discipline.

## Formation of Rule of Law in Corporate Governance

A string of corporate failures sparked the spread of the Asian financial contagion to Korea.[36] One of the many outgrowths of the crisis was

---

34. Supreme Court, Judgment of March 24, 2002.

35. Hasung Jang and Joongi Kim, "Nascent Stages of Corporate Governance in an Emerging Market," *Corporate Governance: An International Review* 10 (2002): 94–105.

36. In March 1997, the Sammi Group, in April, the Jinro Group, in October,

a widespread need to implement reform. Many considered that the government had lost control of the economy and failed to curb the excesses of the chaebol and banks, leaving Korea vulnerable to the contagion. As a result, the banking, financial, and corporate sectors were entirely overhauled. For the first time, significant market-based reforms—such as stronger investor rights, open market for corporate control, total access for foreign ownership, stricter accounting standards, tougher disclosure requirements, and effective bankruptcy procedures—were all established. Checks and balances were put in place to maintain effective management of companies and banks. Rule of law in corporate governance appeared to be slowly emerging.

### Reforms in the Aftermath of the Crisis

Boards of directors now actually hold meetings and even record minutes of their meetings. Outside directors are now required for all listed companies. In large companies, nominating committees, audit committees, and compensation committees are required. Annual general shareholder meetings at which meaningful information is provided are becoming common. Directors face far more scrutiny and disclosure requirements have been dramatically expanded.

Investors, stakeholders, and reputational intermediaries now are far more actively involved in the corporate governance process. They not only question management, but also seek to assert their voting rights and voice their demands. Shareholders have even brought shareholder derivative actions and have prevailed. Yet this type of activism is still uncommon. Management rarely is held accountable through the "hard" legal system. Soft checks and balances continue to be the norm, with tremendous deference given to managerial decisionmaking. Complicating this emerging legal framework is the fact

---

the Kia Group and Ssangbang Wool Group and in November, the Newcore Group fell in succession. Half of the top thirty chaebol would ultimately collapse during the abrupt crisis. Banks collapsed as well and Korea First Bank (KFB), Cho Hung Bank, and Seoul Bank were nationalized in the process.

that the government maintains an active presence that cannot be ignored.

### Stronger Enforcement Mechanisms

The Korea Fair Trade Commission (KFTC) has been consistently at the forefront in public enforcement of laws related to the corporate governance of large conglomerates. The KFTC was established in 1980 to promote fair competition. Another primary goal was to constrain the excesses of the chaebol that dominated the economy.[37] Beginning in 1986, the KFTC began to focus specifically on "economic concentration" issues. The KFTC first sanctioned the largest chaebol for improper related-party transactions in 1998. Following the first investigation in 1998, the KFTC imposed strong corrective measures and levied 74 billion won in civil penalties. After two investigations in 1999, 20.9 billion won and 79 billion won were levied in civil penalties as well.[38]

Under a controversial law, the KFTC also restricts the aggregate investment of the leading chaebol.[39] The law seeks to curtail the vast network of cross-shareholding within large conglomerates. The law restricts the amount of capital contributions that companies within a conglomerate can make to affiliated companies. Companies that are part of conglomerates with at least 5 trillion won in total assets cannot own shares in other affiliates when aggregated together it would exceed 25 percent of their net assets in value.[40] Due to its controversial nature, the law's future hangs in the balance.

The KFTC also prohibits direct cross-holdings of shares between affiliates and guarantees for affiliates.[41] The prohibition applies to

---

37. Monopoly Regulation and Fair Trade Act. KFTC became an independent agency directly under the Prime Minister's office in 1994.

38. The civil penalty cannot exceeding ten per cent of the amount in violation.

39. Article 10 of the Act.

40. Application of this law was briefly suspended between 1998 and 2000.

41. Article 9 of the Act.

enterprises belonging to business groups that have total assets of at least 2 trillion won. The former restriction prohibits an enterprise from owning the shares of an affiliate that in turn owns the shares in the enterprise itself. The latter restriction prohibits an enterprise from guaranteeing the loans made by affiliates from a domestic financial institution.

Finally, the KFTC also regulates holding companies that are defined as those whose total shares in subsidiaries amount to at least 50 percent of their total assets and whose total assets are worth at least 100 billion won.[42] A holding company that violates the regulations can face a civil penalty up to 10 percent of the amount of the total contribution in violation.[43] A holding company must report to the KFTC within 30 days of the registration of the incorporation of the holding company. Despite the apparent success of the KFTC, it could be argued that its public enforcement has been more effective because of its lack of discretion. The KFTC's actions involve straight application of the law.

Another promising development in public enforcement involves the activities of the Korea Deposit Insurance Corporation (KDIC). Since the crisis, the KDIC has aggressively pursued liability against senior managers much in the fashion of the U.S. Federal Deposit Insurance Corporation. It has filed civil actions and injunctions to freeze assets. In 1999, for example, KDIC filed civil liability actions against 222 executives from 53 financial institutions for a total of 263.1 billion won, and it filed 1,560 injunctions to freeze 274.7 billion won. In 2000, the KDFC filed civil actions against 1,287 executives from 157 financial institutions for a total of 5 trillion won, and it filed 1,812 injunctions to freeze 670 billion won in assets of allegedly liable former executives, and it filed 1,812 injunctions to freeze 670 billion won in assets of allegedly liable former executives. The KFTC has

---

42. Article 8 of the Act.

43. Generally, see Christopher Hale, "Addressing the Incentive for Expropriation within Business Groups," Fordham International Law Journal 30 (2006): 1–44.

taken the most far-reaching regulatory actions to hold corporate executives accountable for their decisions, and they are unprecedented
in their scope and severity. Of course, its mandate remains limited
and only applies to failed companies that have received public funds.

In terms of private enforcement, collective action problems served
as a considerable barrier to legal action. Shareholder derivative actions
were still rare. To rectify this and enhance investor protections, in
late 2003, Korea adopted securities-related class actions. Securities-
related actions for market manipulation, accounting fraud, and insider
trading have been subject to class action suits since 2005.[44] Protec-
tive devices have been installed to prevent abusive and frivolous litigation. For instance, for the first year, class actions were limited to
companies with more than 2 trillion won in assets. Unfortunately, the
substantive application of the law was suspended for another two
years, until 2007.

## Conclusions

Against this general background, many significant events occurred
that demonstrated the power of the state and the general rule of man.
In the postauthoritarian era, Korea has undergone widespread legal
change. With market forces gradually taking hold as a result, the
moral hazards of "too big to fail" no longer seems to hold true. Companies have become more transparent and accountable. Rule of law
in corporate governance has slowly emerged. Korea, however, failed
to learn from its mistakes in its postauthoritarian transition toward a
market-oriented economy. The most significant legacy of postauthoritarian legal reforms is the importance of minimizing direct state intervention in the economic realm while providing effective market-
based checks and balances.

Government action must be based upon the rule of law and due

44. Dae Hwan Chung, "Introduction to South Korea's New Securities-Related
Class Action," *Journal of Corporation Law* 30 (2004): 165–180.

process. Market-oriented discipline must exist so that corporations can operate honestly and effectively and not as vehicles for malfeasance, corruption, or expropriation. Korea is at a stage of the formation of rule of law machinery in corporate governance. A natural evolution was hindered because of the legacy of strong state. The rule of law must now prevail as the efficacy of rule of man has largely expired. For corporate governance to operate effectively, a comprehensive legal environment must exist. The lax excesses that followed the postauthoritarian rule, in which neither effective state nor market control could be found, must become relics of the past. Corporate governance founded upon the rule of law must be in place for an efficient, competitive, and disciplined market-based advanced economy to emerge.

## Bibliography

Black, Bernard S., Barry Metzger, Timothy O'Brien, and Young Moo Shin. "Corporate Governance in Korea at the Millennium: Enhancing International Competitiveness." *Iowa Journal of Corporation Law* 26 (2001): 537–608.

Choi, Stephen J. "Law, Finance, and Path Dependence: Developing Strong Securities Markets." *Texas Law Review* 80 (2002): 1657–1727.

Coffee, John C. Jr. "Do Norms Matter? A Cross-Country Evaluation." *University of Pennsylvania Law Review* 149, no. 6 (2001): 2151–2177.

Coffee, John C. Jr. "Privatization and Corporate Governance: The Lessons from Securities Market Failure." *Journal of Corporation Law* 25 (1999): 1–39.

Chang, Seung Wha. "The Role of Law in Economic Development and Adjustment Process: The Case of Korea." *International Law* 34 (2000): 267–288.

Chung, Dae Hwan. "Introduction to South Korea's New Securities-

Related Class Action." *Journal of Corporation Law* 30 (2004): 165–180.

Fischel, Daniel R. and Michael Bradley. "The Role of Liability Rules and the Derivative Suit in Corporate Law: A Theoretical and Empirical Analysis." *Cornell Law Review* 71 (1986): 261–297

Fuller, Lon L. *The Morality of Law* rev. ed., New Haven and London: Yale University Press, 1969.

Gevurtz, Franklin A. "The European Origins and The Spread of the Corporate Board of Directors." *Stetson Law Review* 33 (2004): 925–954.

Graham, Edward M. *Reforming Korea's Industrial Conglomerates.* Washington, D.C.: Institute for International Economics, 2003.

Hahm, Chaihark. "Law, Culture, and the Politics of Confucianism." *Columbia Journal of Asian Law* 16 (2003): 253–301.

Hale, Christopher. "Addressing the Incentive for Expropriation within Business Groups: The Case of the Korean Chaebol." *Fordham International Law Journal* 30 (2006):1–44.

Huh, Young. "Konggwonnyoke uihan Kukje Group haech'eui wibopsong (The Illegal Break-up of the Kukje Group through Public Authority)." *P'allyewolpo* 280 (1994): 16.

Jang, Hasung and Joongi Kim. "Nascent Stages of Corporate Governance in an Emerging Market: Regulatory Change, Shareholder Activism and Samsung Electronics." *Corporate Governance: An International Review* 10 (2002): 94–105.

Johnson, Simon, Rafael La Porta, Florencio Lopez-de-Silanes, and Andrei Shleifer. "Tunneling." *American Economic Review* 90 (2002): 22–27.

Jwa, Sung-hee, and Chan-guk Huh. "Risk and Returns of Financial-Industrial Interactions: The Korean Experience." *Korea Economic Research Institute (KERI) Working Paper* 9801 (1998).

Kim, Hyung Tae. "Legal Market Liberalization in South Korea: Preparations For Change." *Pacific Rim Law and Policy Journal* 15 (2006): 199–231.

Kim, Joongi. "The Judiciary's Role in Good Governance in Korea." *Policy and Society* 26 (2007) Issue 2: 15–32.

Kim, Joongi. "Recent Amendments to the Korean Commercial Code and Their Effects on International Competition." *University of Pennsylvania Journal of International Economic Law* 21 (2000): 273–330.

Kim, Konsik, and Joongi Kim. "Revamping Fiduciary Duties: Does Law Matter in Corporate Governance?" in *Global Markets, Domestic Institutions: Corporate Law and Governance in a New Era of Cross-Border Deals*, edited by Curtis J. Milhaupt, 372–399. Columbia University Press, 2003.

Kraakman, Reinier H., Hyun Park & Steven M. Shavell. "When are Shareholder Suits in Shareholder Interests?" *Georgetown Law Review* 82 (1994):1733

La Porta, Rafael, Florencio Lopez-de-Silanes, Andrei Shleifer, and Robert Vishny. "Investor Protection and Corporate Governance." *Journal of Financial Economics* 58 (2000): 3–27.

Licht, Amir. "Legal Plug-Ins: Cultural Distance, Cross-Listing, and Corporate Governance Reform." *Berkeley Journal of International Law* 22 (2004): 195–239.

Milhaupt, Curtis J. "Property Rights in Firms." *Virginia Law Review* 84 (1998): 1145–1194.

Noland, Marcus. *Avoiding the Apocalypse: The Future of the Two Koreas*. Washington, D.C.: Institute for International Economics, 2000.

Peerenboom, Randall. "Let One Hundred Flowers Bloom, One Hundred Schools Contend: Debating Rule of Law in China." *Michigan Journal of International Law* 23 (2002): 471–544.

Potter, Pitman B. "Legal Reform in China: Institutions, Culture, and Selective Adaptation." *Law and Social Inquiry* 29 (2004): 465–495.

Rowe, Thomas D. Jr. "The Legal Theory of Attorney Fee Shifting: A Critical Overview." *Duke Law Journal* 4 (1982): 651–680.

Sakong, Il. *Korea in the World Economy*. Washington: Institute for International Economics, 1993.

West, Mark D. "Information, Institutions, and Extortion in Japan and the United States: Making Sense of Sokaiya Racketeers." *Northwestern University Law Review* 93 (1999): 767–816.

Yang, Chang Soo. "The Judiciary in Contemporary Society: Korea." *Case Western Reserve Journal of International Law* 25 (1993): 303–313.

Yoon, Dae Gyu. "New Developments in Korean Constitutionalism: Changes and Prospects." *Pacific Rim Law and Policy Journal* 4 (1995): 395–418.

Youm, Kyu Ho. "Libel Laws and Freedom of the Press: South Korea and Japan Reexamined." *Boston University International Law Journal* 8 (1990): 53–83.

*Court Cases*

Supreme Court, Judgment of December 26, 1997, 97 Do 2609.

Seoul District Court, Judgment of Apr. 20, 1998.

Supreme Court, Judgment of March 24, 2002.

Supreme Court, Judgment of March 15, 2002.

Suwon District Court, Judgment of December 17, 2001, 98 Gahap 22553.

Seoul District Court, Judgment of August 20, 1999, 98 Kohap 504.

Seoul High Court, Judgment of October 17, 2002, 99 No 2359.

CHAPTER SIX

# The Rule of Law and Competition Policy in Korea: Transition from a Developmental State to a Market Economy

Wonhyuk Lim

## Introduction

The absence of the rule of law is widely regarded as a critical impediment to economic growth. In particular, the experiences of underdeveloped and socialist economies over the past several decades have shown that the protection of private property and voluntary contracts is essential to economic development.

Yet despite a weak tradition for the rule of law, a number of developmental states in East Asia achieved rapid economic growth. For instance, in Korea, the government exercised a great deal of discretionary power in the name of industrial policy, especially in the early stages of development. During the developmental dictatorship period from 1961 to 1987, the authoritarian government made rules; the idea of binding the government through law was a rather foreign concept. Although the government's preoccupation with economic growth and outward-oriented industrialization served as a partial check on its power, the protection of private property and voluntary contracts in Korea during this period was fraught with uncertainty.[1]

1. In fact, the authoritarian government came to power through a military coup in 1961, and one of its first actions was to arrest "illicit wealth accumulators," business leaders who had profited from their connections to the corrupt Syngman Rhee

However, as the political and economic side effects of "governing the market" became clear, "the rule of law" became an increasingly relevant concept in Korea. One of the most significant developments in this regard was the enactment of the Monopoly Regulation and Fair Trade Act (MRFTA) at the end of 1980. Previous efforts to introduce competition law (or, more broad fair trade law) had failed on several occasions due to strong opposition from the business community as well as the widespread perception of the law as a potentially problematic regulation hampering entrepreneurship and economic growth. The first competition law in Korea was introduced in 1975, but it was enacted as part of a price control measure. As a result, the law had a fundamental contradiction. On the one hand, the law sought to improve efficiency by promoting competition and relying on market mechanism; on the other hand, by controlling prices, the law suppressed price signals essential to efficient resource allocation. After the limitations of the government-managed economy became clear in the aftermath of the heavy and chemical industry (HCI) drive, the government enacted the MRFTA. This shift in emphasis from industrial policy to competition policy was a precursor to a more fundamental transition from a developmental dictatorship to a democratic market economy in Korea.

## The Rule of Law: Conceptual Issues

Before looking at the development of the rule of law and competition policy in Korea, it is probably wise to define how the term "the rule of law" is used herein. For this purpose, it is necessary to define the meaning of "law" first.

The dictionary definition of law is "rule made by authority for the

---

regime (1948–1960). These business leaders were let go only after they promised to support the new government's ambitious economic development plans through donations of industrial plants as well as their entrepreneurial efforts. Business leaders throughout the development dictatorship period were acutely aware that displeasing the government could have serious business *and* personal consequences.

proper regulation of a community or society or for correct conduct in life." This definition contains two elements. On a formalistic dimension, law is "rule made by authority," and on a value dimension, law is what is "proper" and "correct." This dual meaning of law seems to exist in many languages.[2] If we focus on the formalistic dimension, "even a bad law is a law"—a remark Socrates allegedly made as he accepted his death sentence and a quote frequently cited by the authoritarian government in Korea during the darkest days of the dictatorship. The rule of law in this sense has mostly to do with the issue of compliance and enforcement. If we focus on the value dimension, however, law is Law with a capital L, reflecting what is right and just. It transcends political authority. The rule of law in this sense has to do with the restraint of power through what is right and just. From this perspective, political control through rules arbitrarily introduced by authority is little more than the rule of man through law, not the rule of law.

Based on the notion of what is right and just, the rule of law consists of three essential elements: restraint of power, protection of inalienable rights, and procedural legitimacy.[3] The first element is based on the idea of binding political power through law. As such, the restriction of government discretion is the central idea. This is typically based on constitutionalism, through which rights and duties based on an implicit social contract are spelled out. It also requires that the the judiciary be independent from the other branches of government. Ultimately, citizens should be on guard against the rise of arbitrary power.

The second essential element of the rule of law is the protection of inalienable rights. What passes for "inalienable rights" may not be universal, but if the restraint of power through law is the central idea,

2. On this point, see George P. Fletcher (1996), *Basic Concepts of Legal Thought* (Oxford: Oxford University Press).

3. See Barry M. Hager (1999), *The Rule of Law: A Lexicon for Policy Maker* (Tokyo: Mansfield Center for Pacific Affairs).

then the content of law must include some notion of the rights of the individual. The American Declaration of Independence, for example, stipulates that life, liberty, and the pursuit of happiness are basic human rights. To this list, economic rights, such as the protection of private property and voluntary contracts, may be added.

The third essential element of the rule of law has to do with procedural legitimacy. Having great laws on paper is not enough. The application of law should be consistent and fair, ensuring equal treatment regardless of class, race, and religion. The legislative and judiciary process should be transparent in the eyes of those affected by law. Legal enforcement should also be effective and efficient.

When using the term "the rule of law" in connection with competition policy, this chapter primarily focuses on the notion of restricting government discretion during Korea's transition from a developmental dictatorship to a democratic market economy. The protection of "inalienable rights" and procedural legitimacy are secondary concerns within the scope of this chapter.

## Failed Efforts to Introduce Competition Law in Korea

On four separate occasions, in 1964, 1966, 1969, and 1971, efforts were made to introduce competition law in Korea, but none of these attempts proved successful. There were many reasons for the failure of these efforts, including strong opposition from the business community. Ultimately, however, the problem was that the introduction of competition law would have clashed with the government-managed economy during this period.

There were basically three catalysts for legislative efforts to introduce competition law in the 1960s and 1970s: hard-core cartels, abuses of market dominance, and general price inflation. For example, the 1964 legislative attempt was prompted by the so-called three-powder scandal of 1963, in which a few large producers of cement, flour, and sugar had colluded to drive up prices. In 1968, the National Assembly conducted an audit and discovered that Shinjin Motors, then a monopoly importer-producer of automobiles, was making huge profits. The draft bill on regulating monopoly introduced in 1969 was in response to such abuse of market dominance. By contrast, legislative efforts in 1966 and 1971 were largely in response to inflation.

The four draft bills tended to focus on regulating the behavior of dominant firms instead of taking a structural approach to promote competition. For example, the draft bill in 1969 sought to regulate only the harm from monopoly instead of addressing the problem of monopolization by adopting structural remedies, such as divestiture, or the breakup of a monopoly firm engaged in exclusionary conduct.

On each of the four occasions, the business community put up strong resistance. Business leaders argued that it was premature to introduce competition law, as it would place considerable restrictions on the behavior of Korean firms. They added that the law would hamper entrepreneurship and economic growth. And although the Economic Planning Board initiated efforts to introduce competition law, other government bodies, such as the Ministry of Commerce, were much more receptive to the concerns of the business community.

There was also a fundamental contradiction between competition law and the government's general economic policy in this period. This contradiction basically explains why the government focused on regulating the behavior of dominant firms instead of promoting competition and macroeconomic stabilization. In the early stages of development, Korea had established "a government-business risk partnership," through which the government shared the default risks of private-sector firms.[4] This government protection against bankruptcy, however, encouraged firms to undertake aggressive investment as they discounted downside risks. In order to maintain economic stability, the government thus found itself forced to intervene in the

4. See Wonhyuk Lim (2001), "The Evolution of Korea's Development Paradigm," ADB Institute Working Paper (Tokyo: Asian Development Bank Institute).

investment decisions of private-sector firms and place caps on the overall level of investment. Toward this end, the government typically limited entry into major industrial sectors such as automobiles. The government also protected the domestic market and adopted a loose monetary policy in order to improve the profitability of Korean firms and reduce their debt burden.

Consequently, although the fundamental solution to the problem of monopolization and collusion would have been to promote competition by scrapping entry barriers, the government was reluctant to take such action, for it would entail the overhaul of the government-managed economic system. As long as the Korean government subscribed to *gwanchi*, or the rule of government officials, it had to make do with regulating the behavior of dominant firms. Similarly, although the solution to inflation would have been to tighten its monetary policy, the government felt that it had to maintain a pro-producer bias to facilitate rapid capital accumulation, as indicated in Table 1. Again, regulating the behavior of dominant firms was the compromise solution to the problem.

## The Price Stabilization and Fair Trade Act of 1975

The fundamental contradiction between competition law and *gwanchi* was reflected in the Price Stabilization and Fair Trade Act of 1975. The act represented the first successful attempt to introduce competition law in Korea, but it was a strange mixture of price controls and provisions against unfair trade and anticompetitive practices.

In the aftermath of the first oil crisis, the government adopted extensive price controls under the 1975 act. Price regulation of about 150 monopolistic and oligopolistic producers continued until 1979. The government thus suppressed price signals essential to efficient resource allocation while seeking to promote competition and rely on market mechanism, at least in principle. By the end of the 1970s, it had become clear that stopgap measures designed to regulate prices would not work.

Table 1. Investment Growth, Inflation, and Interest Rate Trends
(1964–1978) (Percent Per Annum, Percent)

| | Growth Rate of Investment | Rate of Inflation | Interest Rate on Bank Loans | Interest Rate on Curb Loans in the Informal Sector |
|---|---|---|---|---|
| 1964 | 13.3 | 30.0 | 16.5 | 61.80 |
| 1965 | 19.3 | 5.8 | 18.5 | 58.92 |
| 1966 | 84.0 | 14.6 | 26.0 | 58.68 |
| 1967 | 25.2 | 15.9 | 26.0 | 56.52 |
| 1968 | 52.3 | 16.1 | 25.8 | 56.04 |
| 1969 | 45.1 | 15.5 | 24.5 | 51.36 |
| 1970 | 11.3 | 15.5 | 24.0 | 50.16 |
| 1971 | 24.9 | 12.5 | 23.0 | 46.44 |
| 1972 | 3.7 | 16.7 | 17.7 | 39.00 |
| 1973 | 40.7 | 13.6 | 15.5 | 33.24 |
| 1974 | 30.2 | 30.5 | 15.5 | 40.56 |
| 1975 | 24.9 | 25.2 | 15.5 | 47.88 |
| 1976 | 77.1 | 21.3 | 16.1 | 40.47 |
| 1977 | 43.1 | 16.6 | 15.0 | 38.07 |
| 1978 | 45.1 | 22.8 | 17.1 | 41.70 |

Source: Bank of Korea, Economic Statistics Yearbook and Financial Statements Analysis, various issues

## The Monopoly Regulation and Fair Trade Act of 1980

On the last day of 1980, the Monopoly Regulation and Fair Trade
Act was enacted. The MRFTA was modeled after competition laws
in Germany and Japan and covered all of the principal competition
policy problems: monopolistic behavior, anticompetitive mergers, cartels, and unfair trade practices. However, the Act was more than a
conventional competition law based on the concepts of economic
efficiency and consumer welfare. Concern about large aggregations of
private power was one of the primary factors underlying the enactment of the MRFTA. Concern about feudal practices that harmed
small producers, such as subcontractors, also played a role. As a result, the MRFTA had a multidimensional objective: "to encourage
fair and free competition by preventing the abuse of market-dominating position and excessive concentration of economic power and

by regulating undue collaborative acts and unfair trade practices, thereby stimulating creative business activities, protecting consumers, and promoting the balanced development of the national economy." Although this chapter focuses on the competition section of the MRFTA, the broad scope of the act should not be overlooked.

The MRFTA was passed by the Emergency Committee for National Security, the organization General Chun Doo Hwan's new military regime set up after it declared martial law, disbanded the National Assembly, and banned all political activities. The enactment of the MRFTA was a response to the serious difficulties the Korean economy faced in 1980. The government's ambitious heavy and chemical industry drive and excessive intervention in the 1970s had driven the economy to the verge of a debt crisis. Extensive and prolonged price controls severely hampered the price mechanism and created substantial distortions. This experience prompted a reappraisal of the way the economy was run and led to a consensus that a fundamental shift in policy orientation was necessary. The government under General Chun's rule adopted macroeconomic stabilization measures to fight inflation. It also began to take liberalization measures, abolishing direct price controls and opening trade and investment.

Another significant factor in the legislation, however, was Chun's political need to initiate reforms in accordance with his slogan of "social justice," part of his cynical attempt to gain popular support after having seized power through a military coup and a bloody suppression of the prodemocracy movement. In the aftermath of the HCI drive, there was a growing concern about the dominance of the chaebol, Korea's family-based business groups that had benefited enormously from favorable policy-oriented loans in the 1970s. Chun's regime sided with this popular sentiment and incorporated sociopolitical goals into the MRFTA, such as protecting small producers from feudal business practices and preventing the undue concentration of economic power. The MRFTA was thus presented as a symbol of political commitment to ensuring fairness as well as to improving economic efficiency and promoting consumer welfare.

The competition section of the MRFTA primarily consisted of the following provisions: prevention of the abuse of market-dominating position; prohibition of anticompetitive practices; and prohibition of unfair trade.

Article 3-2 of the act prohibited any "market-dominating enterprise" from engaging in the following abuses of its position: unreasonably fix, maintain, or alter the prices of goods or services; unreasonably control the sale of goods or services; unreasonably interfere in the business activities of other enterprises; and parallel behavior in price increase. The MRFTA required that the Korean Fair Trade Commission (KFTC) designate "market-dominating enterprises" each year in accordance with two market-share criteria: a single firm with a market share of more than 50 percent and two or three firms with a combined market share of more than 70 percent (as long as each individual share exceeded 5 percent) in a market with total domestic sales of more than a certain amount.

The designation of market-dominating enterprises based on their market share amounted to making an irrefutable inference of dominance if a firm satisfies one of the criteria while ruling out a finding of dominance for all others—even if they could exercise market power with a smaller market share than the threshold as defined in the MRFTA.

Moreover, Article 3-2 prohibited not only exclusionary conduct but also "unreasonable" monopolistic pricing and output restriction, and it authorized the KFTC to impose price and output directives as remedial measures. Until 1998, pricing by a market-dominating firm was regarded as "unreasonable" if its price changes were out of proportion with changes in market demand and supply or costs of supply or if its sales expenses and general overhead expenses were excessive compared with the "normal level" in the relevant or comparable market. This attempt to limit "excessive" price increases reflected the perceived need for price controls in concentrated markets, similar to the regulatory approach that had been adopted for the Price Stabilization and Fair Trade Act of 1975. However, the application of the law in this manner involved the difficulty of determining the "proper" level of prices and output for a profit-maximizing firm. To address the problem of monopolization and exclusionary conduct, it would have been better to prescribe structural remedies such as divestiture instead of placing behavioral restrictions based on government discretion.

Article 7 of the MRFTA prohibited mergers that would substantially restrain competition in any line of business. However, Article 7 provided for statutory exemptions for anticompetitive mergers if the KFTC found it necessary to rationalize an industry or strengthen international competitiveness. This proviso gave the KFTC substantial discretion in merger decisions.

With respect to collusion, the MRFTA required that parties to a restrictive agreement register it with the KFTC for prior approval. Unlike in countries with a long tradition of antitrust, in which collusion is illegal except for a few special cases such as cooperative research and develoopment, the MRFTA thus adopted something of a "government management" approach. There were also statutory exemptions for cartels formed for the purpose of overcoming economic depression and facilitating industrial rationalization.

In addition, the MRFTA prohibited practices "likely to harm fair trade" in the following categories: unreasonable refusal to deal and discrimination; unreasonable exclusion of competitors; unreasonable inducement or coercion of competitors' customers to deal with oneself; unreasonable exploitation of one's bargaining position[5]; dealing with others on conditions that unreasonably restrict their business

---

5. Subsequently, a separate statute was enacted to prohibit unfair trade in subcontracting. The Subcontract Transactions Act of 1984 required that the contractor deliver to the subcontractor a written contract and offer reasonable subcontracting prices and conditions.

activities and hindering others' business activities; and unfair practices in labeling and advertising. The notion of "unfair trade" was rather ill-defined in the MRFTA. The concepts of unsportsmanlike conduct, discriminatory treatment, opportunistic behavior, and exploitation prohibition were present to a varying degree for each of the conduct categories, yet their connections to economic efficiency and consumer welfare were not thoroughly investigated.

As a result, the prohibition of "unfair trade" ran the risk of leading competition authorities astray, making them focus on possible harm to trading partners and competitors rather than potential injury to economic efficiency and consumer welfare. For example, a new entrant may engage in innovative sales promotion activities to take business away from incumbents, but the entrant's promotion activities that increased competitive pressure on incumbents might be judged as "unreasonable inducement or coercion of competitors' customers." This kind of misconception regarding the notion of "unfair trade" was not unique to Korea.[6] However, because the MRFTA placed such emphasis on fairness, the potential for misjudging efficiency-improving or competition-promoting practices as "unfair trade" was greater in Korea. Although this problem was not directly connected with the problem of restraining government discretion, it had the effect of muddying the competition section of the MRFTA.

## Subsequent Amendments and Developments

The problems that had initially plagued the application of the MRFTA were subsequently addressed through amendments and other changes in the direction of restricting government discretion. The KFTC became increasingly receptive to structural solutions as the limitations of behavioral restrictions became clear. Also, industrial policy considerations were phased out, as they began to be seen as

6. For the case of the United States, see Robert H. Bork (1978), *The Antitrust Paradox: A Policy at War with Itself* (New York: Basic Books).

impediments to economic restructuring, especially in the wake of the 1997 economic crisis.

With regard to the abuse of dominance, a February 1999 amendment abolished the registration system for market-dominating enterprises. Instead, the amendment required the KFTC to determine the presence of dominance when a case is brought to its attention, considering such factors as market share, barriers to entry, and the relative size of competitors. Although the amendment did not scrap behavioral restrictions altogether, it did abolish the provision that based the judgment of abuse on a market-dominating firm's "excessive" sales expenses and general overhead expenses compared with the "normal level" in the relevant or comparable market. Instead of placing restrictions on the profit-maximizing behavior of the firm, the possibility of using structural remedies such as divestiture to address the problem of monopolization has been finding more support in recent years.

The February 1999 amendment also changed the provision on mergers. Industrial policy considerations, such as industrial rationalization and international competitiveness, were scrapped. Instead, in order for an anticompetitive merger to receive exemption, merger-specific efficiencies should outweigh the harmful effects of reduced competition, or the merger should involve a failing company whose assets would go underutilized or should result in anticompetitive mergers. This change was in line with the increasing competition advocacy role of the KFTC. In fact, the Omnibus Cartel Repeal Act, enacted in January 1999, removed legal exemptions for 20 cartels under 18 statutes, remnants from the heyday of *gwanchi*.

In the same year, the legal standard for anticompetitive practices was changed from "substantial restraint of competition" to "unreasonable restraint of competition," which means that it is no longer possible to defend a restrictive agreement on the grounds that it has insignificant actual effect. In line with international best practice, the new standard reflects the KFTC's intention to apply a per se rule to naked agreements to fix prices, limit output, rig bids, or allocate markets.

Clearly in contrast to the approach taken by the government in the 1970s, these developments show that Korea has come a long way from the developmental dictatorship period, when "the rule of law" was a rather foreign concept. There has been a marked shift in emphasis from industrial policy to competition policy, increasingly relying on market mechanism rather than "the rule on government officials."

# CHAPTER SEVEN

# Institutionalizing Property Rights in Korean Capitalism: A Case Study on the Listing of Samsung Life

Sang-young Rhyu

## What Is Happening with Property Rights in Korea?

The history of capitalism is about the history of property rights. Property rights are the most basic economic institution of capitalism and define who owns and controls property. Therefore, whether property rights are clearly delineated or protected is a barometer of the development of capitalism. In other words, political and economic conflicts within a society to establish or change economic institutions are basically interests regarding property rights. In the history of capitalism, institutional changes regarding property rights have been made mainly in two ways. One, political and social conflicts occur that newly delineate existing property rights or distribute them; and two, efforts for institutional changes to preoccupy potential property rights that would be newly created as a result of technological innovation are put into action.

Korea is one country where property rights have not been firmly institutionalized because there are insufficient institutions to delineate and protect private property. Worse, the rule of politics has more influence than the rule of law when an economic player exercises recognized property rights. In many cases, political consideration plays a big part in distributing values that are newly created out of existing property rights. Accordingly, they are infringed upon or weakened. In particular, large conglomerates (*chaebols*) have grown rapidly in Korea, with the idea of stakeholder capitalism prevailing, disputes over property rights of conglomerates have been on the rise.

Korea has recently witnessed two conflicting phenomena concerning property rights. One, the offspring of those who have been criticized for their activities in favor of the Japanese during colonial rule from the early 1900s have won their lawsuits to recover their ancestors' property. They have reclaimed assets (through legal processes) that the government took from them after the liberation from the Japanese in 1945, based on the principle of protection of property rights. In Korea, there is a political view and a strong nationalist criticism that some pro-Japanese were given property rights in an unjust way from the Japanese colonialist government in the early 1900s and that therefore their property rights should be cancelled by the new government. However, the court has delivered the decision in favor of descendants of pro-Japanese under the principle that property rights should be protected in a capitalist society. When it comes to an individual's property rights in Korea, the rule of politics has lost power while the rule of law has gained strength.[1]

In the meantime, majority shareholders of conglomerates have recently donated their personal assets to society instead of taking responsibility for their mismanagement of companies and their personal corruption. The duties of majority shareholders are detailed in the relevant laws, including commercial law and corporation law. In reality, however, shareholders have evaded their responsibilities in many cases by donating their personal assets to society. Take the Samsung Group's decision to donate 800 billion won and Hyundai Motors' donation of 1 trillion won to society. Such actions show that property rights in relation to the management of a stock company can

1. However, as criticism against the verdicts has escalated, the National Assembly has recently organized the Committee on Inspection of Assets of Pro-Japanese Koreans, and passed an act to get their assets back. (*Hankyoreh*, August 27, 2006)

be weakened under political decisions rather than under a legal and institutional framework.

These two conflicting cases demonstrate that property rights in Korea have not been delineated in a clear way. They also reflect the economic-political power structure over the developmental trajectory of Korean capitalism and the property rights system. In other words, the rule of politics and the rule of law regarding capitalist property rights still exist together. What causes the disparity between the rule of law and the rule of politics? Why do conflicting phenomena occur and how are they resolved?

This chapter analyzes the factors that help delineate and change property rights in Korean capitalism. Specifically, I would like to take the initial public offering (IPO) of Samsung Life Insurance (SLI) and related debates to find the political and economic reasons for its continued delay.[2] An IPO is a process that delineates a stock company's property rights and requires a complicated political mechanism. The listing of SLI not only shows the developmental trajectory of the property rights system and the mechanism for reforms in Korea, but also provides theoretical suggestions for the future direction of Korea's capitalist economic institutions.

Then, I review existing approaches toward property rights and the characteristics of Korean capitalism focusing in particular on the nature of the firm and the origin of disputes over property rights. Next, I briefly describe the development of property rights throughout the history of Korean capitalism, in particular examining major events that helped establish property rights. In addition, I review and reinterpret a few examples of property rights being weakened or infringed in Korea since the 1970s.

In the next section, I clarify the origin of attempts to list stocks of SLI along with the resulting developments as well as relevant dis-

---

2. In November 2009, Samsung Life Insurance finally announced its plan to go public in the first half of 2010.

putes and power coalitions (the reason their IPO has been delayed is explained by spelling out the pros and cons of the issue and policy coalition). And finally, I explore the role of the government and politics in this issue, emphasizing that the government might not be the final protector of property rights. Additionally, I discuss the role of property rights in reforming corporate governance in the future and consolidating democracy. In conclusion, I stress the need to institutionalize and depoliticize property rights for the development of Korean capitalism and democratic consolidation.

## Theoretical Overview of Property Rights and Korean Capitalism

An IPO is an institutional process that delineates and distributes property rights in a firm. Why choose SLI as an example from amongst so many firms? There are several reasons for using this case to approach changes in property rights in Korea from a perspective of political economy. First, SLI is a de facto holding company of Samsung Group, the biggest *chaebol* in Korea. As such, it has great influence on the whole group and the overall Korean economy. Second, SLI represents the developmental trajectory and characteristics of the Korean financial market and the major economic institutions. Characteristics of the Korean financial market, which is relatively underdeveloped, and the government's financial policies have been reflected in the life insurance market, major institutions and policy ideas surrounding SLI. Third, SLI is at the center of efforts to reform corporate governance that has been processed rapidly since the financial crisis in 1997. How SLI will be listed will decide the ownership structure of the whole Samsung Group. This is significant because it will be the last stage of corporate reform that has taken place in Korea. Last, disputes concerning the IPO of Samsung Life Insurance will be resolved through political reasoning and compromise because many interested parties have divergent interests in the issue. As issues become a matter of politics, the operation and confrontation between policy coalitions with conflicting interests definitely become political and strategic. In this regard, the IPO of Samsung Life Insurance is a good case that shows that all processes of institutional changes, including delineation and redistribution of property rights, are the result of political games.

Existing research on property rights can be divided into two categories. From an economic perspective, property rights are already exogenous and private. The traditional approach came from the liberalism of John Locke and the *Wealth of Nations* by Adam Smith. The key questions were how to distribute or delineate property rights efficiently while avoiding "the tragedy of the commons" by rational individuals and the function of market. Even under the economic perspective, however, there is no ideal property right that can be applied under any and all circumstances. Nevertheless, it was concluded that private ownership is more desirable than public ownership. "Certain public works" that liberal economists, including Adam Smith, mentioned also play the role of facilitator to expand private ownership of free enterprises. Today, economists focus their research on a firm as the product of contracts among parties in the market to delineate property rights. Studies on corporate governance that have recently attracted attention also deal with delineation and use of property rights.

Meanwhile, the other from a political perspective, property rights are endogenous variables. Property rights have been an important topic in the political process and the role of government has been emphasized as a tool to delineate and distribute property rights. Accordingly, the role of government has been analyzed as the definer or enforcer of property rights that could correct the market failure. Most of the research has not taken the role of government for granted. Rather, they have paid attention to how and why the role of government has been highlighted. Under the condition that the government is authorized to use violence lawfully, there was a state-centered interpretation that "might makes rights." However, there is no objection that it is very naïve to assume that government, with its monopoly on force, will perform optimally.[3] Then what does "the government" mean herein? It means law. Jeremy Bentham, a representative utilitarian, said government's direction had the upper hand over individual decision, emphasizing that property rights cannot exist without government.[4] In particular, he underlined the role of law, saying, "Property and law are born together and die together. Before laws were made there was not property; take away laws, and property ceases."[5] However, utilitarians rarely mentioned in detail how law is made and how property rights are changed.

Then are property rights created or evolved without reason? Property does not just happen and evolve. From an economic perspective, the size of potential profit out of the delineation of property rights and the transaction costs necessary for establishing contracts among individuals are major variables in the creation of and changes to property rights. In particular, the emergence of an entrepreneur who can sense individual profits from open access and wants to realize them would cause changes to property rights. Then from a political perspective, how should the origin and evolution of property rights be explained? In addition, how is the cost-benefit analysis in economics reflected in the political process to change property rights?

These questions are the starting point of this examination. Property rights can be declared more rapidly by the government. However, the government's decisions about property rights arise out of the power relationship among political coalitions. The delineation and execution of property rights by the government can either protect or destroy property rights. Therefore, the role of government can be either a just regulator of property rights or an outright taker of existing rights. After all, the role of government is decided through struggles among policy coalitions with conflicting interests over the delineation,

---

3. McChesney 2003, p. 9
4. Bentham, Jeremy, *Theory of Legislation*, London: Trubner, 1882
5. McChesney 2003, p. 15

distribution, and execution of property rights. In this regard, I focus on the political process amongst policy coalitions, its outcome, and the role of government concerning the IPO of Samsung Life Insurance.

A firm is the most developed institution in a capitalist society. It is an economic institution comprising property rights established amongst individuals and relevant contracts. However, even in a firm, property rights are never perfectly delineated. With respect to delineation and disputes of property rights within a firm, A.C. Pigou dismissed the role of private property rights and argued that government regulations are more effective.[6] In contrast, Ronald Coase insisted that private property and bargaining are more effective as long as the transaction costs are excessively big.[7] Adolph Berle and Gardiner Means argued in *The Modern Corporation and Private Property* that the core of a modern company's property rights is the separation of ownership and control. In other words, property rights of a company are scattered, making it difficult for those who own the company to effectively possess it. Rather, those who run the company but do not own it enjoy the benefits of the property.

Therefore, disputes over a company's property rights can be summed up in this question: "Who claims the rights of residual rights?" The fact that the owner and the manager are not one and the same prevents the profit-maximization paradigm of economics from working properly in a firm. Resolving the problem and overcoming its limits require debates and relevant analysis.

The concept of property rights, or "who owns what," can be divided into three categories. First, economic property rights enable one to spend relevant assets and are delineated by economic principles. Second, legal property rights are rights over the relevant property and are recognized and executed by law. Third, political property rights

6. Pigou, A., *The Economics of Welfare*, London: Macmillan, 1932
7. Coase, Ronald H., "The Problem of Social Cost," *Journal of Law and Economics* 3 (October), 1960, pp. 1–44

can be argued politically and, accordingly, changed or redistributed under political situations.[8] Based on economic property rights and legal property rights, existing assets can be exercised and protected. They also help maintain property rights in a stable manner. However, political property rights can be newly delineated or distributed depending on political circumstances or the reformation of policy coalition. Therefore, political property rights are a more convenient tool for analyzing changes to property rights.

Irrespective of differences over property rights, they are maintained in a stable manner as long as there are not any disputes. The government and politics play the role of regulator or protector of property rights, whereas the rule of law becomes a major principle for the execution of property rights.[9] However, when disputes occur, the rule of politics has more influence than the rule of law. So when do disputes arise? Disputes happen mainly for the following three reasons: First, in a market or technology-driven case, the emergence of new technologies or markets gives rise to new property, and disputes occur when attempts are made to delineate it. Second, in a private interest-driven case, disputes occur when an individual attempts to change another individual's property rights or public goods under his/her private interest. Third, in a politics-driven case, disputes occur when attempts are made to redelineate, divide, or redistribute existing property rights following changes of political circumstances or emergence of a new political coalition. In general, however, disputes concerning property rights occur because of a combination of the three forms of rights. And in the case of a contract that does not clearly delineate some rights whose value has increased, a conflict may emerge as well.[10]

    8. Barzel, Yoram. *Economic Analysis of Property Rights*. Cambridge: Cambridge University Press, 1997, pp. 3–15.

    9. North, Douglas C. *Institutions, Institutional Change and Economic Performance*. Cambridge: Cambridge University Press, 1990.

    10. Williamson, Oliver E. *The Economic Institutions of Capitalism*, New York: Free Press, 1985.

## Historical Development of Property Rights in Korean Capitalism

Since Japanese colonial rule, the development of Korean capitalism has been led by the state: The government has delineated and redistributed private property rights, and the market and civil society have not raised strong objections. Under the developmental strategy for enhancing national wealth and the export-oriented industrialization policy by the authoritarian regime in the 1960s, governmental influence over private property rights has become stronger.[11] However, as the regime's economic policies brought about economic growth, the market and civil society started to make stronger demands for market autonomy and for easing regulations on the market. In addition, the economic growth led to increased demands for democratization. This provided momentum for new changes to the overall government-business relationship. Eventually, the political and economic environment around property rights since democratization in 1987 changed "from a secure autocracy to an insecure capitalism."[12] In other words, property rights had been politically protected or fixed by the authoritarian regime, but as democratization progressed, conflicts over property rights were on the increase. Demands for reclaiming infringed or deprived property rights and for new property rights broke out suddenly.[13]

In the meantime, the evolution of property rights is related to the development history of Korean conglomerates. Companies were tra-

11. Barzel, Yoram. *Economic Analysis of Property Rights*. Cambridge: Cambridge University Press, 1997, p.97.

12. There are many ways in which governments can violate—or fail to protect from private theft and usurpation—the property and contract rights of their citizens and subjects: direct expropriation of assets, defaulting on public debt, debasing the currency, prohibiting any transactions other than those at officially established prices, and failing to provide a legal infrastructure that impartially enforces contracts and adjudicates disputes about property rights. (Clague, "Property and Contract Rights in Autocracies and Democracies," *Journal of Economic Growth*, June 1996, 254.)

13. Olson, 1996

ditionally managed and owned by families. With the emergence of big businesses after the 1970s, however, capitalism evolved to so-called managerial capitalism.[14] Accordingly, conflicts over property rights and the necessity of redistribution increased as related corporate governance and new institutional arrangements for property rights were required.

In the history of Korean capitalism, property rights have been gradually delineated and strengthened. However, they also have been infringed or weakened. For example, in the 1910s, imperialist Japan conducted surveys of arable lands. From an economic institutional perspective, this can be interpreted as an occasion that helped delineate modern ownership of arable lands.

From 1948 to 1951, the Rhee administration carried out land reform by confiscating assets inherited from the colonialist rule period and assets of landowners with compensation and distributed these assets to farmers. This was the first transformation of property rights since the liberation of the country. The purpose was to abolish the landlord class, create the small farmer class, and transform land capitalists to industrial capitalists.

In the early 1960s, President Park Chung-Hee adopted modern economic policies to promote industrialization, notably, a variety of corporate laws. In general, Anglo-American law and Japanese law were adopted. Economic institutions that were introduced at this time dealt with basic rules necessary for delineating and distributing corporate property rights.

In the mid-1980s, in the meantime, the Chun Doo Hwan regime privatized many public corporations. Privatization that transferred the ownership of public corporations from the government to private investors is a process that distributes or delineates property rights of a country to the civil sector. Therefore, it carried significance in the development of property rights in Korean capitalism.

14. Long-lasting democracies generally provide better property and contract rights than either transie

Since then, the government has continued to implement privatization policies. Economic reforms that took place rapidly after the financial crisis in 1997 brought about substantial change to institutions concerning property rights. In particular, property rights that had been vaguely delineated or incorrectly distributed were newly delineated and redistributed through reform of the corporate and public sectors. Specifically, institutions for the separation of ownership and control and the protection of minority shareholders' interests were strengthened. In summary, this is a new delineation of residual claims. All these processes can be interpreted as a historical event through which property rights were institutionalized by the market as Korean capitalism developed.

Meanwhile, private property rights have been violated or weakened by state intervention and as a result of conflicts of political interests. The so-called August 3 Measure, announced unexpectedly by the Park Chung Hee administration on August 3, 1972, is a representative case that property rights were infringed. With an aim to support large conglomerates suffering from inefficient management and heavy financial costs, the government forced creditors to convert private loans to stocks and thus made changes to individual property rights. As a result, Korean chaebol succeeded in escaping from the pressure of debts, but individual creditors' property rights were under severe threat.

In February 1985, the Kukje Group was dismantled under the Chun Doo Hwan administration's restructuring plan. A predominant interpretation of the event is that the political rule played an important role in the event. In many cases, corporations and groups were disorganized when they failed to establish a cooperative relationship with the new regime.[15] In many cases since the 1997 financial crisis, majority shareholders of big businesses have announced that they

15. Chandler, Alfred. *Scale and Scope: The Dynamics of Industrial Capitalism.* Cambridge: Harvard University Press, 2004.

would donate their personal wealth to society in acknowledgment of
their mismanagement of companies and in response to society's criticism. For example, CEOs of groups such as Daewoo, Samsung,
Hyundai, SK, and LG donated personal property to society. However,
this did not originate from altruistic motives. Rather, this was caused
by the pressure of public opinion and political compromise. Therefore, it can be interpreted that property rights were damaged under
political logic. Since CEOs were majority shareholders by commercial
law, all they could do was to take responsibility for their mismanagement as shareholders and managers. However, they were forced to
donate their personal assets irrespective of their limited responsibilities as stated in the relevant laws. Worse, if they were to take responsibility for their wrongdoing, they were supposed to make compensation to their companies and guarantee shareholders' profits.
Instead, they donated their assets to society. This definitely shows
that both the government and society have not fully protected property rights. This is also a barometer of the institutionalization level of
property rights in Korea. Table 1 shows the major cases of contributions of private chaebol money in which property rights were infringed or attenuated in the history of Korean capitalism.

So why do property rights continue to be weakened despite the
development of capitalism and the institutionalization of property
rights in Korea? What are the decisive variables that delineate property rights? The analysis of the listing of Samsung Life Insurance case
shows that power relations among political coalitions, rather than economic policies, delineate property rights.

## The case of the listing of Samsung Life Insurance Corp.

### Origins and development of SLI case

The case of the SLI listing stemmed from the government decision
in the mid-1980s to provide more blue-chip stocks to facilitate the

Table 1. Major Cases of Contributions of Chaebols' Private Money

| Date | Who | Case/Amount of Money |
|------|-----|---------------------|
| August, 1972 | Private creditors | 8.3 measures (for companies to be exempted from private debts) |
| June, 1980 | Dongmyung Timber (Kang Seok-Jin) | Forced to break up & donate land to the government. |
| February, 1985 | Kukje Group (Yang Jung-Mo) | Forced to break up by Chun regime |
| April, 1999 | Daewoo Group (Kim Woo-Choong) | Payed off KW 1 trillion & offered KW 10 trillion as security. |
| May, 1999 | Samsung Group (Lee Kun-Hee) | President Lee forced to give $2.5 billion to creditors for Samsung Motors' failure |
| June, 1999 | Choyang Group (Park Nam-Kyu) | Donated approximately KW 30 billion for failure of Choyang Merchant Marine |
| April, 2000 | Hyundai Group (Chung Ju Yung's family) | 3136 of Hyundai's affiliates sold & made to donate $5.2 billion. |
| May, 2000 | Saehan Group (Lee Jae-Kwan) | Payed off KW 24 billion for management failure. |
| March, 2003 | SK Global (Choi Tae-Won) | Pressed to contribute KW 106 billion for cooking the books. |
| January, 2004 | LG Group (Koo Bon-Moo) | LG Corp & major affiliates sold after the LG Card failure. |
| April, 2006 | Hyundai Motor (Chung Mong Koo's family) | Declare a plan to donate KW 1 trillion for a series of scandals. |

premature stock market. At a time when good corporations were rare, the Korean government attempted to expand the stock market and help corporations with their financing by listing stocks of life insurance companies. Through several rounds of meetings, the Ministry of Finance announced in April 1989 that SLI was suitable for being listed. In August 1990, the ministry offered "the guidelines for the distribution of surplus and revaluation reserve" as a preparatory measure to list SLI stocks. Based on the guidelines, SLI carried out asset revaluation on the condition that stocks would be listed. Despite a series of discussions about the method of listing, it has been postponed for many reasons, including the bearish stock market. The exemption period for asset revaluation reserve was also postponed several times.

In 1999, the issue of SLI emerged again. Facing financial crisis, Chairman Lee Kun-Hee of the Samsung Group donated W2.8 trillion worth of SLI stock to creditors for the failure of Samsung Motors. After the exemption period for asset revaluation reserve expired, the SLI listing was discussed again in 2003. However, due to different perceptions on the characteristics, the decision to go ahead with the listing was postponed one more time.

After the financial crisis in 1997, it became essential for Samsung Motors to repay debts in order to complete its restructuring plan. For this reason, the SLI listing appeared to be a realistic option. Before the financial crisis, the listing of the company was promoted as a way of facilitating the stock market. Now, however, it was considered to be a solution for the bad loans of Samsung Motors. Ever since Chairman Lee donated SLI stock in 1999 as part of the effort to solve the Samsung Motors issue, the Samsung Life Insurance problem has been discussed more frequently.

However, in December 2000, the Financial Supervisory Service (FSS) decided to postpone the final conclusion. Accordingly, the creditors of Samsung Motors submitted a listing proposal to the FSS in November 2002. The FSS reported the proposal to Kim Dae Jung's Presidential Transition Team in January 2003. As for the Kim Dae Jung administration, it saw that resolution of the Samsung Motors problem should be implemented as a way of enhancing the effectiveness of the corporate restructuring plan. Finally, the head of the Financial Supervisory Commission (FSC) started to review the case in May 2003. The following June, the newly established Advisory Board for the Listing of Insurance Companies held hearings; 11 political organizations, economic institutions, and civil organizations in attendance. In August, a variety of discussions and consultations took place regarding the way listings were made. On October 17, 2003, however, the FSC and the advisory board concluded that the listing was postponed because "compromise between interested parties is deemed to be difficult, and the legal basis is not clear."[16]

As the creditor banks of Samsung Motors filed a lawsuit against Samsung's 28 affiliated companies on December 9, 2005, for compensation of losses in the amount of KW 4.7 trillion and for interests, the SLI listing came under discussion yet again. The creditors of Samsung Life Insurance originally expected to collect bonds by selling donated stocks once they were listed on the stock market. However, when the listing did not make any progress with accumulated losses, creditors decided to resolve the matter in court. Samsung's legal representatives argued that the contract with the creditors of Samsung Motors in 1999 was forced under political pressure and thus was invalid.[17]

On the contrary, creditors said that the contract was made voluntarily through the decision of the board of directors of Samsung. With the listing of Samsung Life Insurance delayed, the debt of Samsung Motors has become a legal issue. In January 2006, the Korean government and the Korea Exchange decided to establish the Advisory Commission on the Listing of Samsung Life Insurance under its organization and to introduce measures to list life insurance companies on the stock market based on the current Stock Market Listing Regulation. On July 13, 2006, the commission ruled that life insurance companies could go public since they were stock companies.[18]

16. Jwa, Sung-hee. *The Evolution of the Chaebols: The Property Rights System and Economic Organization in Korea: A New Paradigm for Korea's Economic Development.* New York: Palgrave, 2001.

17. Advisory Board for the Listing of Insurance Companies, *Position on the Listing of Life Insurance Companies* October, 2003.

18. In October of 2005, Jong-young Yun, CEO & Vice Chairman of Samsung Electronics said at the inspection of the administration by the Commission on Finance and Economy of the National Assembly, "Chairman Lee has no legal respon-

However, this is not a final decision or a consensus-based measure. Therefore, more arguments and confrontations are expected to come out in the future.[19]

### Conflicting Issues and Power Coalition

There are three main issues concerning the SLI listing: the characteristics of Samsung Life Insurance, the asset revaluation reserve, and the division of profits arising out of the listing.

As for the characteristics of life insurance companies, civil groups argued that Korean life insurances companies were mutual companies and not stock companies because they have sold insurance products with dividends for more than 30 years since their establishment. In addition, the overall management risks have not been dealt with by shareholders only, but by shareholders and policyholders together.[20] Meanwhile, life insurance companies said that they were stock companies established by shareholders' paid-in capital under commercial law and the Insurance Business Act. While the decision to offer insurance products with dividends was made by management and arose from the government's encouragement, policyholders have never shared the management risks. Therefore, policyholders do not have voting rights whereas shareholders do.[21]

---

sibility but has donated personal assets to society from the moral point of view," hinting that he would not accept creditors' demand (December 2, 2005, *Joongang Daily*).

19. Advisory Board for the Listing of Insurance Companies, *IPO of Life Insurance Companies*, www.krx.co.kr; (July 13, 2006; *Maeil Business Newspaper* (July 13, 2006)

20. The chairman of the Advisory Board, Dong-min Na (research fellow of the Korea Development Institute) said in an interview that a few issues remain to be reviewed and some revaluation assets should be distributed to policy holders, adding "it is desirable to offset stocks of Samsung Electronics owned by policy holders with those of shareholders of Samsung Life Insurance before the IPO (*Economy Plus*, 2006, 152–154).

21. People's Solidarity for Participatory Democracy (PSPD) has actively presented its view. In particular, its economic reform center deals with the issue. In the website of PSPD (www.peoplepower21.org/article), a series of articles have been posted, including those of civil groups' view on the positions of the government and Samsung Life Insurance.

Second, civil groups insisted that capital surplus out of asset re-valuation was the contribution that policyholders made. Therefore, the surplus should be distributed to policyholders in the form of stock. Life insurance companies took the position that although reserved money was dealt with in the capital account, it was reserved in effect for policyholders who are creditors. Therefore, dividends should be distributed to them in the same way ordinary profits are distributed.

Third, civil groups said that the listing should be allowed on the condition that capital surplus from the listing be redistributed to policyholders in the form of stock or cash. Life insurance companies said that distribution of capital surplus is against the principles of a stock company and an attempt to do this is infringement of shareholders' property rights. They said that this was also against the constitution.

After all, according to civil groups, Korean life insurance companies, including Samsung Life Insurance and Kyobo Life Insurance, are mutual companies, not stock companies. Therefore, policyholders have the same voting rights as shareholders have and capital surplus from the listing should be redistributed to them. Failing that, they argue against the listing of life insurance companies. Meanwhile, under the logic of life insurance companies, they are stock companies in which policyholders do not have voting rights and do not have the right to redistribute the surplus out of the listing. In other words, all capital gains from the listing should be enjoyed by shareholders only. All of these conflicting options can be summed into one question: Who owns the residual rights? In other words, will shareholders have the residual claims or will shareholders and policyholders share them? It is also a question of whether property rights and the increased economic value of a company whose stock was listed on the stock market should be protected or redistributed. In brief, the existing shareholders say that property rights should not be divided or violated, whereas policyholders want them to be distributed.

The divergent position on the listing of life insurance companies has given rise to two conflicting policy coalitions over this issue. One argues that it should not be listed unless it meets the condition that the capital surplus should be distributed to policyholders. The other insists that the capital surplus should be distributed exclusively to shareholders. The former is "the antilisting coalition" based on stakeholder capitalism and the latter is "the prolisting coalition" based on shareholder capitalism.

The stakeholder-based coalition consists of civil groups, including the People's Solidarity for Participatory Democracy (PSPD), the Citizens' Action Network, the Citizens' Coalition for Economic Justice (CCEJ), labor organizations, including the Korean Confederation of Trade Unions (KCTU) and the Federation of Korean Trade Unions (FKTU), and progressive politicians whose main concern is policyholders' interests because policyholders are the political base. The stakeholder-based coalitions emphasize that life insurance companies are the products of the government-oriented industrialization policies, that they are not companies established by shareholders, and that within a mutual company, policyholders have shared the management and thus their voting rights and rights to profits should be respected. Civil groups and labor organizations have attended public hearings concerning the listing of life insurance companies and made efforts to strengthen policyholder activism and accomplish their goals.

With a common voice of policyholders yet to be formed, civil groups have represented them. Concerning labor organizations, the labor unions of life insurance companies have made their efforts to carry out their missions with the support of their national organization. Samsung Life Insurance does not allow an official labor union, so workers fired by the company and individual employees have participated in the movement. In the meantime, progressive politicians have exerted political influence over the issue to gain political support at public hearings and during the deliberation on relevant bills so that profits can be redistributed to policyholders. Beneath their percep-

Figure 1. Conflicting Coalition-Building

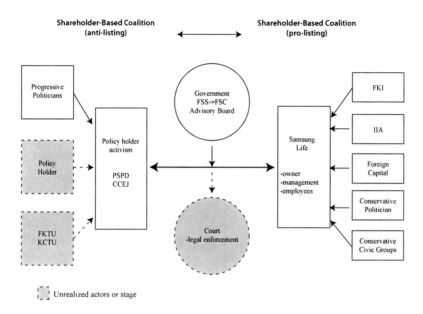

Unrealized actors or stage

tions lie the strategies to appeal to the public, which has a critical view of the chaebol, including Samsung. So the government has no option at the moment but to take the public into consideration.

Meanwhile, the shareholder-based coalition comprises shareholders, employers and employees of Samsung Life Insurance as well as those working in the life insurance industry, international capitals, conservative politicians and civil groups. First, all shareholders, employers and employees of Samsung Life Insurance want their company to be listed so that they can obtain substantial economic profits from the IPO. For example, employees can have unlisted stock and can receive more stock through the Employee Share Ownership Program. By excluding policyholders from the profit distribution, they can increase their profits. Conservative politicians and civil groups have taken their position in order to establish capitalism in Korea through which shareholders are respected and their property rights are protected.

Only shareholders should share profits when life insurance companies are listed on the stock market, given that they form a strong ideological and policy coalition with capitalists or managers' organizations. For example, the Federation of Korean Industries (FKI) wants to establish a strong policy coalition that can nullify progressive politicians or labor unions. In addition, international capitalists want life insurance companies to be listed as soon as possible so that they can seize new business opportunities in Korea, launch into the Korean life insurance market, and make investments there. Under the idea of the so-called global standard, they have become a powerful partner to establish shareholders' capitalism and strengthen their property rights. The International Underwriting Association (IUA), representing the Korean life insurance companies, has also argued that shareholders' profits should be reserved. It has even put pressure on the Korean government in its policies.[22]

As indicated above, the government has repeatedly adopted the policy to mediate positions of the two sides and encourage them to compromise. Specifically, the government has focused on gathering opinions and checking differences through the establishment of the FSC Advisory Board for the Listing of Insurance Companies. In other words, the government has not made specific decisions on the issue. Rather, it has evaded the risk of policy failure by responding sensitively to the ups and downs of the stock market depending on political environment in Korea. No one has asked for a final legal decision on the matter. The creditor banks of Samsung Motors have recently filed a lawsuit to recover their bonds. However, this is not an attempt to make judicial judgment on the listing issue. In this regard, neither has obtained the upper hand. They don't want to take responsibility

---

22. Samsung Life Insurance, *Review on Issues Related with the IPO of Life Insurance Companies*, unofficial inside material, 2004.

for making a legal decision. They have just waited to see how the matter has developed over time.

## Politics, Law, and Chaebol Reform in the Samsung Group

### Government and the Rule of Politics

As conflicts between divergent policy coalitions have continued, the listing of life insurance companies has been delayed. The government has not made its official decision on the issue either. The views that the Advisory Board for the Listing of Insurance Companies and the FSC suggested during their meetings with related organizations in August 2003 are based on the rule of politics, not on the rule of law.

The advisory board's views can be summarized as follows: First, there is no legal authority to distribute to policyholders any capital surplus of a listing. Second, asset revaluation reserve can be related to profit distribution; that requires more review, but, there are insufficient institutional regulations on this matter. Third, due to the legal limitations, distribution of profits from a listing can be decided by the compromise of interested parties. On October 17, 2003, the advisory board finally announced that it was not going to make any decision or suggest any proposal in the resolution of the matter. In the materials distributed for a hearing on July 13, 2006, the advisory board insisted that insurance companies be considered stock companies and that "whether dividends were distributed to policy holders in a proper manner in the past should be reviewed with various factors."[23]

The government's compromising attitude originates from its practice of resolving disputes concerning property rights through political bargaining. For example, the KFTC recommended in 2004 that the

---

23. As three out of nine members of the Advisory Board for the Listing of Insurance Companies belong to accounting firms, outside auditors of life insurance companies, there have been criticisms that the advisory board can be free from the industry. (*Hankyoreh*, July, 24, 2006)

SLI listing should be allowed on the condition that it would contribute 15 percent of the profits from the listing to establishing a nonprofit foundation. The FSC has also suggested that Samsung Life Insurance donate W1.5 trillion upon its listing as a public fund.

More interesting, Samsung, like the government, has also decided its strategies and behaviors based on rule of politics. The Samsung Group would have the advantages it needs by listing Samsung Life Insurance. First of all, it could pay the debts of Samsung Motors, and Samsung's shareholders and employees would enjoy enormous marginal profits. Officially, Samsung Life Insurance wanted to list its stocks on the stock market as soon as possible on the condition that the profits from the listing would not be distributed to policyholders. This corporate strategy has been confirmed several times as policies have been made. However, the Advisory Board for the Listing of Insurance Companies has found that while preparing to make the final decision, Samsung Life Insurance's view on the issue changed abruptly. In other words, Samsung Life Insurance and Kyobo Life Insurance had insisted consistently that their stocks be listed as soon as possible. However, they made it clear, while the Advisory Board prepared for the final report on the fall of 2003 that "it would not intend to list their stocks following the proposal by the Advisory Board for the Listing of Insurance Companies." Discussions could not progress because of this.

Apparently, Samsung Life Insurance, on behalf of the Samsung Group, has changed its view on the listing since it is difficult to oppose the demand of policyholders and civil groups for distribution of profits. In fact, it is likely that the company is concerned about the changes that the listing would bring to the overall governance structure of the Samsung Group. Jeong Han Lee of the Korean law firm Bae, Kim & Lee, one of the members of the advisory board, said, "Samsung has raised its objection to the listing suddenly, which can be linked to the issue of corporate governance structure." (October of 2004, Seoul, an interview on the phone) As indicated in Figure 2,

Figure 2. Ownership Structure and Control of the Samsung Group

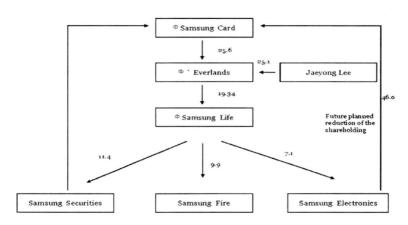

Circular financing Structure through ① → ② → ③ is completed.
* Refers to unlisted compaines.

Samsung Life Insurance has played the role of de facto holding company of Samsung Group. Therefore, the listing of Samsung Life Insurance can lead to big changes to the Samsung Group's governance structure in general. In particular, this can bring about unexpected consequences for the control of Samsung Group by the majority shareholder, the Lee family, the founding member of the group. Moreover, this can affect who will succeed as chairman of the group. For example, if the 3.5 million shares of stock (17.5 percent) of Samsung Life Insurance that the creditors of Samsung Motors have acquired should be traded to other shareholders after the listing of the company, the control of the Samsung Group by Jae Young Lee (son and an assumed successor of Lee Kun Hee), who owns 19.34 percent of the stock and is the majority shareholder of Everland, an affiliate of the Samsung Group, would be weakened.[24] While "families remain the primary beneficiaries of managerial capitalism," the interests and voice of the founding family of the Samsung Group have played the biggest role in the group.[25]

After all, Samsung Life Insurance has not given up its tendency to rely on the rule of politics rather than the rule of law. Above all, it was difficult to ignore social pressure to distribute profits from the listing.[26] Also, the listing was expected to cause enormous reshuffling to the overall governance structure. Given the circumstances, the company has decided to keep the status quo. In other words, the objection of Samsung Life Insurance to its IPO means that it won't redelineate its corporate property rights in legal terms and won't divide or distribute property rights under the current circumstances around which disputes concerning property rights arose. It was a political decision to prevent the infringement of the existing property rights that could happen from the redelineation and distribution of property rights and leave the corporate governance intact at the same time. Of course, the government, including the FSC, has opted for political compromise and decided to keep the status quo as well. In this regard, when the government prefers political compromise and the rule of politics, the state is not necessarily the most efficient protector against all aspects of theft.[27]

24. The Advisory Board for the Listing of Insurance Companies, *The Listing of Insurance Companies*, 2006 (August), p.14.

25. www.pressian.com, *PRESSIAN*, January 31, 2006.

26. Chandler, Alfred. *Scale and Scope: The Dynamics of Industrial Capitalism.* Cambridge: Harvard University Press, 2004, p.492.

27. On February 7, 2006, Chairman Lee of Samsung Group said that he would donate KRW 8 trillion to society and drop lawsuits against the government concerning the revision of Finance Development Act. So-called the national sentiment is reflected Lee's decision, which also shows the political and social reality of Korea. (*Joongang Daily*, February 7, 2006.)

## Rule of Law and Corporate Reform

What should be done to resolve disputes concerning the listing of Samsung Life Insurance and its property rights and finally to delineate and strengthen property rights? The rule of politics should be stopped and the rule of law needs to be strengthened. Under the current political compromise and noninstitutional equilibrium, it is desirable to redelineate property rights and realize institutional equilibrium based on relevant economic institutions and laws.

So why are all relevant parties reluctant to resolve the issue on the basis of the rule of law? The stakeholder-based coalition sticks to the political compromise because they are concerned about damage that will occur when a legal decision is made that Samsung Life Insurance is a stock company. Legal property rights are expected to remain untouched by the political and social pressures. The shareholder-based coalition prefers the rule of law. However, they cannot ignore the effect of the remaining rule of politics, and they are uncertain of the changes that the listing would bring to corporate governance. Against this background, the government has opted for a risk-averse solution. At least in the case of the listing of Samsung Life Insurance, the government has given up its role as definer and enforcer of property rights. The government should suffer legal burdens and criticism that it breaks individual property rights when it prefers the rule of politics and solve the issue by social compromise. On the other hand, if the government chooses the rule of law, it has to incur political burden because it ignores social pressure and national sentiment. Accordingly, the government has tried achieving socialization of defining property rights by making a clear legal regulation that life insurance companies are a stock company and recommending that part of the profits from the listing be distributed to policyholders.

Against the government's decision lies its own inertia: The government has maintained its past attitude despite the economic reform since the financial crisis in the late 1990s. As a result, the rule of law has not run properly. We can find two recent, seemingly confrontational tendencies in the legal process in Korea. One is that the rulings concerning chaebol take time and are prolonged. This is because the court and the government consider political property rights and maintain the old-fashioned attitude, relying on political compromise and trying to solve problems through non-institutional channels. The other is that in the lawsuits, chaebol have raised points against the government concerning financial and competition policy, and the government has lost to chaebol in an increased ratio. This shows the limitation of arbitrary political decisions. This also demonstrates that disputes concerning overall economic issues have been gradually resolved based on the rule of law.

One of the focal points of corporate reform is to clearly delineate corporate property rights and protect them, and by doing so, to remove institutional uncertainty over property rights and enhance institutional rationality and stability. Delineation and practice of property rights within a company is directly linked to corporate governance and thus has been a main dispute of corporate reform in Korea and abroad. On the contrary, disputes over property rights occur because corporate property rights have not been clearly delineated with a poorly performing corporate governance. Currently, there are three main acts regarding the listing of Samsung Life Insurance: (1) The Commercial Act stipulates the requirements for a listing and the subsequent distribution of profits, (2) the Insurance Act stipulates insurance goods and detailed contracts; (3) the Asset Revaluation Act prescribes corporate tax regulations after revaluation after listing. Related laws have been revised and developed as part of economic and corporate reform.[28] However, there is a long way to go before regulations on property rights related to a listing are fully prepared. In

---

28. Barzel, Yoram. *Economic Analysis of Property Rights.* Cambridge: Cambridge University Press. 1997, p.118.

Korea, economic systems related to economic reform are still path-dependent and embedded in the history of financial market development and the developmental state.[29]

How to allocate the disputed property rights? Legal property rights are not disputable. However, when corporate governance and the process of capital accumulation fail to gain much credibility from society, political property rights cannot be completely neglected either. In this regard, Korea is in a transition period from the rule of politics to the rule of law.[30] At the formal institution level, most economic institutions have been reformed according to global standards. However, at the informal-practice level, institutional inertia and cultural embeddedness still have an affect. The role of the government, the listing of Samsung Life Insurance, and the corporate governance of the whole Samsung Group cannot be removed from reality. Therefore, the settlement method incurring the lowest total cost will be selected.

## Conclusion: Institutionalizing Democratic Consolidation in Korea

How can property rights be free from the effect of politics and be institutionalized? Answers to this question will be the barometer in Korea of the development of democracy, the growth of a market economy, and the rule of law. Korea successfully transformed to a democracy in 1987 and has experienced a wide range of economic reforms since the financial crisis in 1997. Currently, Korea is faced with two tasks and challenges: how to consolidate democracy and how to sustain the growth of market economy. Resolution of these matters requires efforts to strengthen institutions of property rights

29. Rhyu, Sang-young and Lee Inkwon, The *Competition Policy and Large Business in Korea*, Policy Paper, Samsung Economic Research Institute (in Korean), 1998.

30. Rhyu, Sang-young and Lee, Seungjoo. "Economic Reform and Changes in Informal Networks between Government and Business in Korea," *Political Science Review in the 21st Century* 16, no.1 (in Korean), 2006.

and remove political and institutional uncertainty. In Korea, where the traditions of stakeholder capitalism and a developmental state remain, the effect of the government and social opinions on property rights will decide whether democracy will be consolidated. In order to fully consolidate democracy, the relations between government power and property rights should be clearly established and operated. Perhaps the question should be rephrased as follows: "How can collective coercive power be harnessed to enforce property rights and the rule of law, without abuse of that same power to disrupt rights?[31] The capitalism of Korea will be upgraded only when property rights are institutionalized and democracy is consolidated by strengthening the rule of law and sustaining the development of the market economy.

## References

Anderson, Terry L., and Fred S. McChesney, eds., *Property Rights: Cooperation, Conflict, and Law*, Princeton and Oxford: Princeton University Press, 2003.

Barzel, Yoram. *Economic Analysis of Property Rights*. Cambridge: Cambridge University Press, 1997.

Barzel, Yoram. "Property Rights in the Firm," In Terry L. Anderson and Fred S. McChesney. 2003.

Bentham, Jeremy. *Theory of Legislation*, 4th ed, London: Trubner, 1882.

Berle, Adolph, and Gardiner Means. *The Modern Corporation and Private Property*. New York: Commerce Clearing House, 1932.

Chandler, Alfred. *Scale and Scope: The Dynamics of Industrial Capitalism*. Cambridge: Harvard University Press, 2004.

---

31. Corporate law is definitely affected by political and social factors. Depending on the combination of politics and law, the corporate law contains different regulations "Law alone does not do as well as law and politics. . . . politics dominates the legal explanations" (Roe, "Corporate Law's Limits" Discussion Paper No.380 (07, 2002), Harvard Law School, p.13, p.37).

Clague, C. "Property and Contract Rights in Autocracies and Democracies," *Journal of Economic Growth*, June 1996.

Coase, Ronald H., "The Problem of Social Cost." *Journal of Law and Economics* 3 (October 1960), 1–44.

*Economy Plus*, August 2006: 152–154.

*Hankyoreh*, July 24, 2006, August 27, 2006

Homepage of Korea Exchange at www.krx.co.kr

Homepage of the Fair Trade Commission at www.ftc.go.kr

Homepage of Financial Supervisory Committee at www.fsc.go.kr/Eng/about/workplan.htm

Homepage of the Ministry of Finance at www.mofe.go.kr

Homepage of the People's Coalition for Participatory Democracy at www.peoplepower21.org

*Joonang Daily*, February 7, 2006

Jwa, Sung-hee, "The Evolution of the Chaebols: The Property Rights System and Economic Organization in Korea," in *A New Paradigm for Korea's Economic Development*. New York: Palgrave, 2001.

Kim, Il Jung, *Property Rights and Regulations* (in Korean). Seoul: Korean Economic Research Institute, 1995.

*Maeil Daily Business*, February 1, 2006

McChesney, Fred S., "Government As Definer of Property Rights: Tragedy Exiting the Commons?" in Terry L. Anderson and Fred S. McChesney, eds., *Property Rights: Cooperation, Conflict, and Law*, Princeton and Oxford: Princeton University Press, 2003.

North, Douglass C. *Institutions, Institutional Change and Economic Performance*. Cambridge: Cambridge University Press, 1990.

Olson, Mancur, Jr. "Big Bills Left on Sidewalk: Why Some Nations Are Rich and Others Poor," *Journal of Economic Perspectives* 10, no. 2 (Spring 1996), pp.3–24.

Pigou, A., *The Economics of Welfare*, 4th ed. London: Macmillan, 1932.

Rhyu, Sang-young and Lee Inkwon. *The Competition Policy and Large*

*Business in Korea* (in Korean), Policy Paper, Samsung Economic Research Institute, 1998.

Rhyu, Sang-young, and Seungjoo Lee. "Economic Reform and Changes in Informal Networks between Government and Business in Korea" (in Korean) in *Political Science Review in the 21st Century* 16, no.1

Roe, M. "Corporate Law's Limits." Discussion Paper No. 380, Harvard Law School (July 2002).

Samsung Life Insurance. Review of Issues Concerning the Listing of Insurance Companies. Unofficial Paper. 2004.

The Advisory Board for the Listing of Insurance Companies. Position on the Listing of Life Insurance Companies (October 2003).

The Advisory Board for the Listing of Insurance Companies. The Listing of Insurance Companies (August 2006).

Williamson, Oliver E. The Economic Institutions of Capitalism. New York: Free Press, 1985.

# CONTRIBUTORS

**Jongryn Mo** is Professor of International Political Economy, Graduate School of International Studies, at Yonsei University, and a research fellow at the Hoover Institution. Professor Mo received his BA from Cornell University and PhD from Stanford Business School. Prior to joining Yonsei University in 1996, he was an Assistant Professor at the University of Texas at Austin. His field of specialization is in international political economy, East Asian development, political economics, and political bargaining.

**David Brady** is deputy director and senior fellow at the Hoover Institution. He is also the Bowen H. and Janice Arthur McCoy Professor of Political Science and Leadership Values in the Stanford Graduate School of Business, and a professor of political science in the School of Humanities and Sciences at the university. He has published seven books and more than 100 papers in journals and books. Among his publications are *Revolving Gridlock: Politics and Policy from Carter to Bush II* (Westview Press, 2006) and *Red and Blue Nation? Characteristics and Causes of America's Polarized Politics* with Pietro Nivola (2007).

**Lee Hoi-chang** was a distinguished visiting fellow at the Hoover Institution, 2003–2004. He is a former prime minister, supreme court justice, and presidential candidate of the Grand National Party in 1997 and 2002.

**Chaihark Hahm** is Associate Professor of Law at Yonsei University. After receiving his BA degree from Seoul National University, Professor Hahm continued his study at Yale, Columbia, and Harvard Law School where he received his SJD in 2000. He then served as a Reagan-Fascell Democracy Fellow at the National Endowment for Democracy before joining Yonsei University in 2002. Professor Hahm's expertise is in constitutional law, Confucian political theory, comparative law and politics, human rights, and religion and politics. He has a forthcoming book tentatively titled "Politics of Relationality: Family and the Public Good in East Asia."

**Hoon Jaung** is Professor of Political Science at Chung-Ang University in Seoul, Korea. His articles on comparative and Korean politics have appeared in Electoral Studies, Journal of East Asian Studies, and other scholarly journals. His current research projects include the future of East Asian cooperation, South Korea's plans to fight corruption, and the dynamics of divided governments in Korea and the United States. He contributes political columns on a regular basis to major South Korean newspapers, Chosun Ilbo, Dong-A Ilbo, and Joong-Ang Ilbo.

**Joongi Kim**   Upon earning his JD from Georgetown University, Professor Kim first practiced law in Washington D.C. at Foley and Lardner. His academic career began in Hongik University and he is now Associate Professor of Law and Associate Dean of International Affairs at Yonsei University. His areas of expertise are international trade law, corporate governance, corruption and financial regulation.

**Wonhyuk Lim** received his BA and Doctoral degrees from Stanford University. Dr. Lim is now a Fellow at the Korea Development Institute. He is a well known expert on big business in Korea and Korean's unification policy. Dr. Lim had provided policy advice to the Korean government on privatization and corporate sector reform as well as inter-Korean relations, and has also served as a consultant to the World Bank and Asian Development Bank Institute. Dr. Lim served as an advisor for the First Economic Subcommittee of the Presidential Transition Committee to the President of Korea after the 2002 Presidential Election.

**Sang-young Rhyu** is Associate Professor of Political Economy, Graduate School of International Studies, Yonsei University. Before joining Yonsei University in 2001, he had served as a senior research fellow at Samsung Economic Research Institute. His teaching and research interests include East Asian political economy, Korean economic institutions, and comparative political economy between Japan and Korea.

# INDEX